THE RIVER YARE:
BREYDON & BEYOND

Sheila Hutchinson

Sheila Hutchinson

Front Cover Photograph: Henry Hewitt, nicknamed 'Yoiton', by the River Yare at
Berney Arms in 1959. Henry Hewitt was the last marshman to operate the Berney
Arms drainage mill. Photograph by Edward Roberts.

Back Cover Photograph: The recently restored Hardley drainage mill in 2009.

ISBN 9780954168377

Published
by
Sheila & Paul Hutchinson
7, Colman Avenue,
Stoke Holy Cross,
Norwich,
Norfolk.
NR14 8NA

Printed
by
RPD Litho Printers
Gorleston
Norfolk

Acknowledgements:

It has been a great pleasure to meet up with people who have lived, worked, and played along the River Yare, having been warmly welcomed into many of their homes for a good old yarn about how it once was. I wish to thank them all.

I wish to express many thanks to the following people for their help in providing valuable information and permission to reproduce photographs, information and tales for this book; without their help this book would not have been possible.

Mrs Joan Adams (nee Humphrey). Mr Peter Allard. Mr John Baker. Mr Ted Brackenbury. Mr Mike Browne. Mr John Burton. Mr Roy Carr. Mr Ron Carter. Mrs Janet Church (nee High). Mr Rod Clarke. Mr Alan Clutten. Mr Malcolm Cushion. Mr & Mrs Arthur & Hilda Edwards. Mr Michael Gunton. Mr David Hewitt. The late Mrs Millie High (nee Hewitt). Mr & Mrs Sonny and Myra Horton. Mr Sid Howlett. Mrs Bridget Jex (nee Saunders). Mrs Julie Layton (nee Debbage). Mr Robert Malster. Mr Ivan Mace. Mr Colin May. Mr Mike Pickard. The late Mr David Pyett. Mr Keith Rackham. Mr Edward Roberts. Mrs Diane Rushbrook. Mr Steve Sanderson. Ms Peggy Sawbridge. Mr Arthur C Smith. Mr Michael Sparkes.

Special thanks go to Paul Hutchinson for all his encouragement, help with research, preparation of sketch plans and maps, scanning of photographs, and the typing of the book for publication.

Every effort has been made to establish copyright for the photographs used in this book but in some cases this has proved impossible. Anyone with a copyright claim is asked to contact the publisher in writing.

Disclaimer:

I have tried to check the accuracy of the information contained in this book but I apologise for any errors that may be present, and I cannot accept responsibility for the consequences of any errors and omissions.

DEDICATION

This book is dedicated to my grandson James Callum Black and my granddaughter Keira Marie Black.

On Breydon Water

INTRODUCTION

I lived at the Berney Arms hamlet by the River Yare from 1946 to 1963. During that time I spent many hours sitting on the river bank watching the cargo boats, lighters, wherries and the Golden Galleon go by. Today there are only cruisers and yachts, and the odd restored wherry that goes along the Yare.

My grandfather Henry Hewitt (Yoiton) of Ash Tree Farm Berney Arms was the last marshman to operate the Berney Arms Mill in 1949. Living in such an isolated place my grandfather had his beer and spirits delivered to Berney Arms from Great Yarmouth by boat.

As I lived in such a remote place by the River Yare I thought it would be interesting to research the mills and pubs further up river.

This book contains information about, and photographs of, the drainage mills and public houses along the River Yare between Breydon Water and the confluence of the River Yare and the River Wensum, and photographs of some of the ships and boats which travelled the River Yare.

SS Annie in the 1930s travelled the River Yare between Norwich and Great Yarmouth delivering beer for Steward and Patteson Brewery.

BREYDON WATER.

Breydon Water is Britain's largest inland tidal water. It is about 4 miles long and one mile wide at its widest point. At low water vast mudflats appear on either side of the navigational channel. These flats are almost all mud brought down river by the Yare and the Waveney and deposited here. The two rivers converge at Breydon Water at about TG471052. The level of the mudflats is fairly uniform except at the edges of the navigational channel where the mud is slightly higher and this causes the water to be retained on the mudflats at low tide and to flow away slowly through natural drains. The mud is usually visible at low tide for about an hour, and is covered by about 3 or 4 feet of water at high tide.

The mudflat is firm enough for walking if great care is taken but the edges of the drains can be soft.

The mudflats provide the food for many species of wildfowl and birds such as the Turnstone, Grey Heron, Oyster Catcher, Redshank and Ringed Plover etc., which feed on the grubs and insects living here. The bird life on and around Breydon Water has over the years attracted many wildfowlers, birdwatchers and naturalists. Arthur Patterson, the naturalist and author spent much time around Breydon and had a houseboat on Breydon. Robin Harrison the naturalist, who wrote for the Gt Yarmouth Mercury, and who became the first Breydon Warden also had a houseboat on Breydon. The RSPB now are the wardens for this nature reserve.

'Firmity', one of the Everard's coasters, passing through Breydon Viaduct in 1947. Supplied by Peggy Sawbridge.

BREYDON WILDFOWLERS

Breydon Water was once a wildfowlers' paradise. During the nineteenth century the wildfowlers shot anything and everything all the year round. They had enormous punt-guns and long narrow punts in which they would lie in ambush awaiting the unsuspecting birds. The common birds they shot would be taken to game shops in Great Yarmouth or elsewhere, and the rare birds would be taken to taxidermists or sold to collectors. Many of the wildfowlers lived in houseboats moored around Breydon Water and they were often known by fancy names such as 'Pintail' Thomas, 'Tapes' Youngs and 'Punt' Palmer.

George Jary, from John Burton

In the 1880s the Wild Birds Protection Act was passed and this prohibited the shooting of any wild birds between 1st March and 1st August. Many of the punt-gunners ignored the new laws so the Breydon Wild Birds Protection Society appointed a 'watcher' to help enforce the laws. The first 'watcher' was 'Ducker' Chambers. Later George Washington Jary was appointed as Breydon Birdwatcher in 1899, and he continued till 1927.

Gradually it became increasingly difficult for the wildfowlers to make a living and the full time professional wildfowler disappeared leaving only part-timers who supplemented their income by other means. The large punt-guns were prohibited in the 1960s and only the shoulder gun is permitted these days.

BREYDON SMELTERS

On Breydon Water at the confluence of the rivers Yare and Waveny a sight no longer seen is the Smelt fishermen. They would have been a regular sight in the nineteenth century and the first half of the last century.

The European smelt, Osmerus Eperlanus, is a small fish typically up to ten inches long, much like a small whiting. The body is long and slim, the head rather pointed and it has a pointed snout. They live in the coastal waters around Europe feeding on shrimps and small crustaceans. They enter the rivers to spawn upstream during the months March to May. Their back is a light olive green, the belly and sides are silver, and they smell like cucumber, sometimes they are known as cucumber fish.

Several families from Great Yarmouth, Cobholm and Burgh Castle once fished for smelts for a living. These included Charlie Carr, Billy Barber, the Frosdicks, Ben Burgess and the Brackenburys, who all fished for smelts during the winter season.

Photograph by P. H. Emerson entitled 'Breydon Smelters' published in 1890.

Fred Brackenbury and his brother Billy, who lived next door, lived at Stepshort, Burgh Castle and had a rowing boat, which they kept at Burgh Castle Staithe, moored in one of the little bays there. They would row the boat across Breydon Water and fished for smelts near Berney Arms. Smelting was a two-man job. Billy stood on the shore holding the rope, which was attached to one end of the net, while Fred would be in the boat and row off, with the net on the stern of the boat, into the deep water where he would run the net over the side of the boat. Fred, too, would have a rope attached to the other end of the net and would make it fast to the boat. He would then row the boat upriver and Billy would walk along the shore with his rope up to a given marked point where Fred would then row ashore and get out with his rope. Together they would haul the net in until it was ashore with the smelts in the net. They would put the catch into a basket, the rope and net were then put back in the boat and they would go back down river and repeat the procedure three or four times depending on the size of the catch and the state of the tide.

The best time for fishing was at the beginning of the flood or the last of the ebb when the tide was slack. The area that was fished was called a 'smelt draft'. There were only certain areas on Breydon that could be worked to get a clear draft so that the net would not get snagged.

The first boat to arrive would get the first draft, and sometimes there would be two or three boats waiting to do a 'rounder', the name they gave to the fishing operation.

The net used by Fred and Billy was about 40 feet by 10 feet with a ¾ inch mesh, by contrast Charlie Carr used a sixty yard long by eight feet deep net. Cork floats were spaced every two feet along the top and small lead weights about six inches apart along the bottom, and a three foot long trammel stick was attached at each end.

Fishing all done Fred and Billy would put their baskets with the catch in the boat and row back to Burgh Castle Staithe where the catch and nets would be unloaded. The nets were hung out to dry on three posts on the riverbank ready for next time. The baskets of fish were put on a barrow and taken along Porter's Loke and back to Fred's house at Stepshort where they would be packed, helped by Fred's sons Allan and Ted, into small wooden boxes, approximately 12 by 9 by 2 inches, each holding about 20 fish. The boxes were made at home and after the lids had been nailed into place the boxes were tied in bundles and the top box labelled. The bundles were then taken to Belton station and put on the 5:30 pm train to London to be sold at Billingsgate Market the following morning.

Smelts were a delicacy favoured by the gentry and would sell for about two shillings a score; this was when the average wage was about two pounds a week.

Charlie Carr's smelt boat was a double-ended boat, about fourteen feet long with a raised floor aft, which was known as a 'thattick' and this was to run the net onto. The boat was also used for eel catching and babbing. Charlie sent his fish from Vauxhall station to Grant and May of Billingsgate

Ben Burgess of Burgh Castle, back in the 1930's, kept his boat in the reeds near Burgh Castle Church Farm. When his nets needed to be repaired they would be taken home and hung on a big nail on the wall in the living room. This was a bit overcrowded with a large family and a room only twelve-foot square. Ben employed a Mr Reader of Burgh Castle to help him when he went smelting, but when times were hard and he could not afford to pay for help his wife Dora or one of his children would go with him. The Burgess family never ate any of the smelts that they caught as they were the main source of income during the winter months. In the net there would also be bream, dabs, mud-butts and eels, which would be eaten by the family or the cat. During the summer months Ben Burgess was a skipper on holiday yachts and at other times he worked in boat yards repairing boats.

Fishing for smelts was a very hard way of making a living, being out in the open with the bitterly cold winds blowing across Breydon Water and the open marshes. Times changed after the Second World War when more motorised river-craft appeared and the faster running tides left no suitable places to work a draft net.

Roy Carr mending his Smelt nets in 1959. Supplied by Roy Carr.

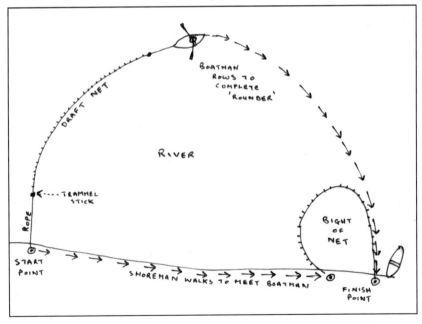

Sketch showing the usual method of Smelt Fishing, often known as doing a 'rounder'.

BREYDON BRIDGE

The railway viaduct over Breydon Water was perhaps the grandest engineering structure on the whole of the Midland and Great Northern Joint Railway network. It was built to connect Yarmouth Beach station with the Great Eastern Railway line from Yarmouth South Town at Gorleston. The Breydon viaduct consisted of five spans, one of which was an opening span which rotated horizontally around its midpoint, creating two 60ft wide clearings for large seagoing ships to pass through. The opening span was on a central pivot of cast iron and moved on circular ball-bearings, 2 inches in diameter

The total cost of the structure was £38,453. Work began in 1899, separate contracts being granted for Foundations and Piers, Superstructure and Hydraulic equipment. On July 8th 1903 the viaduct was tested successfully with a train of heavy engines and it opened shortly afterwards. The bridge had a short life and closed prior to the rest of the M&GN network in 1953. The track remained in situ for several years afterwards and demolition began in 1962.

Work started on the new road bridge over Breydon Water in late 1984. Initially some of the pilings from the old railway viaduct had to be removed as they unfortunately could not be reused as they were in the wrong positions. The new road bridge operates on the cantilever principle and was constructed in the Turmeric yard in Southtown before being floated down river on a barge and raised into position over the duration of one night. The bridge is controlled by an operator in the control room which is positioned on its western side.

COLIN MAY REMEMBERS

My house on Cobholm was a short walk from the marshes and the Breydon Estuary. I've been using gunpunts on Breydon Water for shooting, rowing and sailing from my early teenage years. For many years I owned two gunpunts. The punts were 21 ft. and 19 ft. long and 4 foot at their widest point.

The two punts were kept in a boatshed on the banks of the River Yare at Cobholm. I rented the boatshed from Great Yarmouth Port and Haven at £4 a year. The boatsheds were well over a hundred years old but were demolished in the year 2000 because of continual vandalism and land redevelopment.

Colin May with his gun-punts at Cobholm boatsheds in the 1990s.

Colin May on Breydon Water in a gun punt. Supplied by Colin May

Colin May near the houseboat 'Lapwing'. Supplied by Colin May.

'Princess Elizabeth' on Breydon Water with a Newcastle dredger 'Coquet Mouth' in 1993. Supplied by Peter Allard.

Everard's coaster 'Spontaneity' stuck on frozen Breydon Water on 22nd January 1963. She made regular trips to the Norwich Power Station. She was 163 ft long and had a gross tonnage of 500 tons. Photograph by Peter Allard.

BREYDON WRECKS

The remains of many old vessels are located on Breydon Water. These include:

The remains of the pleasure steamer 'Waterfly' which was beached in the 1930s along the south wall to help protect the Breydon Wall.

The wooden hulled steam drifter 'Ocean Emperor', which for a period of time had moorings at South Quay in Great Yarmouth and was used as a training ship for the Sea Scouts, and was left to rot on the south wall of Breydon.

The wooden steam drifter 'Marie' whose remains were scuttled on Breydon south wall.

Billy Tooley's wherry the 'Widgeon' which sank after being hit by a bomb in 1943 and was raised and towed to the south bank of Breydon.

The remains of four wherries believed to once having been owned by the Burgh Castle Cement Works were scuttled on the north bank in the later part of the nineteenth century.

The wreck of an old brigantine 'Agnes' which was placed on Breydon in 1876 by the Port and Haven Commissioners.

Breydon Bridge 9th September 2006.

'Pinguin' on Breydon
Water in 1938.
Supplied by Peggy
Sawbridge.

Top: Maintenance men on Breydon Bridge on 7 May 2002. Photograph by Peter Allard.

Bottom: Broads Authority launch on Breydon Water on 20 May 2002. Peter Allard.

16

'Admiral Day' on Breydon Water piling in new navigation marker post, 12 April 1999. Photograph by Peter Allard

Lockgate Mill in working order circa 1930. Perry.

PUBLIC HOUSES BETWEEN BREYDON WATER AND TROWSE EYE

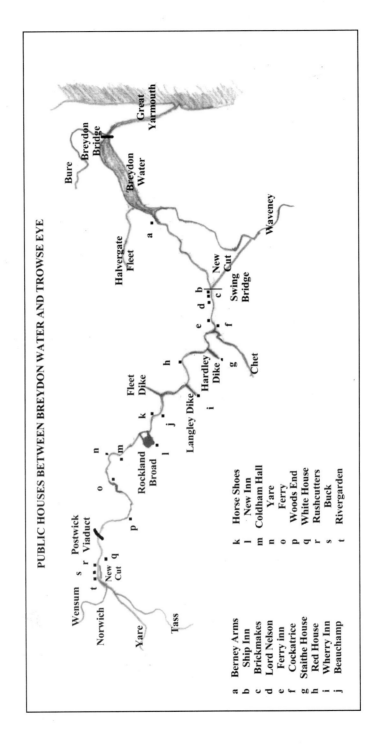

a	Berney Arms	k	Horse Shoes
b	Ship Inn	l	New Inn
c	Brickmakes	m	Coldham Hall
d	Lord Nelson	n	Yare
e	Ferry inn	o	Ferry
f	Cockatrice	p	Woods End
g	Staithe House	q	White House
h	Red House	r	Rushcutters
i	Wherry Inn	s	Buck
j	Beauchamp	t	Rivergarden

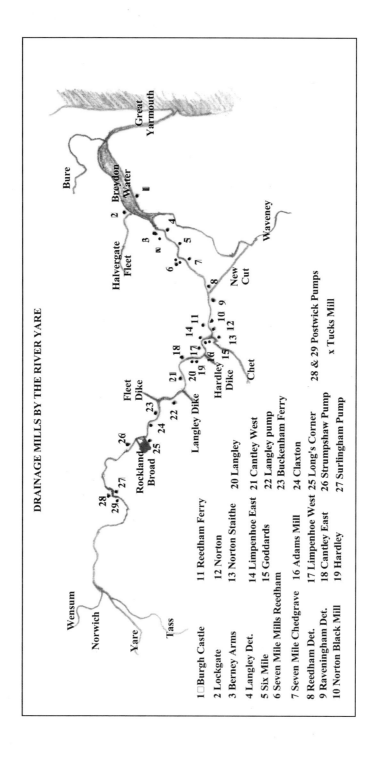

DRAINAGE MILLS BY THE RIVER YARE

1 □ Burgh Castle
2 Lockgate
3 Berney Arms
4 Langley Det.
5 Six Mile
6 Seven Mile Mills Reedham
7 Seven Mile Chedgrave
8 Reedham Det.
9 Raveningham Det.
10 Norton Black Mill

11 Reedham Ferry
12 Norton
13 Norton Staithe
14 Limpenhoe East
15 Goddards

16 Adams Mill
17 Limpenhoe West
18 Cantley East
19 Hardley

20 Langley
21 Cantley West
22 Langley pump
23 Buckenham Ferry
24 Claxton
25 Long's Corner
26 Strumpshaw Pump
27 Surlingham Pump

28 & 29 Postwick Pumps
x Tucks Mill

19

LOCKGATE MILL AND MARSH HOUSE (TG480072)

Located in Freethorpe Detached Parish, Lockgate Mill was also known as **Freethorpe Mill, Banham's Black Mill and Duffel's Mill**. It was not marked on Faden's map of 1797 but was marked on Bryant's map of 1826 as Freethorpe Mill.

The mill is four storeys high, built in red brick and tarred black. The brickwork stands 35 feet high and it is about 24 feet overall diameter at the base and had four windows and two doors. It carried four patent sails, which turned clockwise and drove a large external scoop wheel, 19 feet in diameter with seven-inch wide paddles.

When it was put up for sale in 1877 it was described as 'recently erected by Smithdales of Acle' so the existing mill was probably a rebuild. A small steam engine may have been installed either here or by the Breydon pump in the early 1900's for a time, as Arthur Patterson mentioned such an engine in his book of 1907 and said Dan Banham was the marshman.

Bob Banham operated the mill around 1912 and Gordon Addison, who lived at nearby Lockgate Farm, is believed to have looked after the mill for a time in the 1920's. The mill was last worked in the mid-1940's by Leonard Carter.

'Sale by auction at Royal Hotel, Norwich, October 6th 1945:

Lot 3. The valuable freehold marshman's occupation known as Lockgate Mill situated in Freethorpe detached & adjoining Breydon Water, containing 79a 3r 17p. This comprises: sitting room with slow combustion stove, kitchen with cooking range, Dairy and 3 bedrooms. Brick and tiled wash-house with iron pan & sink, small boarded and tiled stable, lean-to coal house and wood & corrugated Iron Open Shed. An excellent brick Tower Mill with patent sails, new water wheel, the whole being in good order together with the following ...(list of marshes) . As in the occupation of Mr B. L. Banham on a yearly tenancy to include the workings of the drainage mill at a rental of £80 0s 0d per annum. (Special Conditions of sale as regards lot 3 as to part thereof with an Indenture of Conveyance dated 13 April 1898 made between Charles Prentis Sarah Prentis and Ellen Prentis of the first part Lauretta Ellen Ann Ravizzotti of the second part Sir Humphrey Francis de Trafford of the third part and Lady Mary Annette de Trafford Charles Edmund de Trafford and Lord Bellow of the third part.')

The mill then remained derelict and the sails were blown down in 1953. A temporary aluminium cap was fitted in 1985, and in November 1988 the mill with the stocks lying on the floor, and the derelict marsh house, then owned by the Banham family, went up for sale by auction with an expected price of £8,000 to £12,000 and was bought by Mr Kim Baker for £16,000. The mill is still owned by Mr Baker, and remains derelict.

The **Marsh House**, which stood next to the mill had a tiled roof and was built of Suffolk whites bricks, and was tarred black the same as the mill. The house had two bedrooms upstairs and two living rooms downstairs. The kitchen was built separate and you had to go outside to get to it. It also had a dairy. There was no electricity and cooking was done with a coal-fired cooking range. Water was obtained from the roof and collected in tanks. The Tithe Map of about 1840 does not mention a marsh house here and so it must have been built sometime later.

LOCKGATE FARM

This large farmhouse was marked on Faden's map of 1797 and on all subsequent maps. It has generally been known as Lockgate Farm or Lockgate House but has also been referred to as 'Duffell's House'. The older part of the building was constructed of small two inch bricks with wrought iron window frames, suggesting it was very old. The rest of the house was built later with the larger bricks. It was a large house with a total of eleven rooms, six of them bedrooms upstairs, and two of them large parlours downstairs. Access to one of the rooms upstairs was only by its own staircase from the dairy.

The house and outbuildings stood till 1981 when everything was demolished. It had stood empty for several years prior to this falling into disrepair and suffering from the effects of vandals.

The original purpose of the building is uncertain. It has been suggested that it was a tollhouse as it was situated on the old drift-way track going from Yarmouth to Halvergate and Wickhampton. The Tithe map has a 'lock' marked by the house but we can only guess at what kind of lock this was. As the course of the Halvergate Fleet and other natural creeks may have changed in the far distant past is it possible that one once entered Breydon near this house and sluicegates or lockgates were once located here.

BREYDON PUMP (TG477070)

The Halvergate Fleet originally entered Breydon water by a sluice gate but a diesel pump was built in 1933 and began to work in 1934. It was capable of pumping 35 tons of water per minute from the Fleet.

The diesel pump was replaced with an electric pump. Work began on the new electric pump in 1946 and the plant, consisting of two motors, was installed by Smithdale & Sons. The new pump was officially opened in October 1948 by Mr H Gardiner of the Ministry of Agriculture and Fisheries, and is capable of discharging up to 138,000 tons of water in 24 hours from the Fleet into Breydon Water. The old green diesel pumphouse still stands alongside the redbrick building holding the electric pump.

Fred Hewitt looked after the diesel pump when he lived at the old Berney Arms pub in the late 1930's and early 1940's. Reggie Mace operated the pump when he worked for Fred Hewitt. 'Yoiton' worked the electric pump after he moved into Ashtree Farm at Berney Arms and he continued to work the electric pump for a couple of years after he moved to Cobholm. Stanley Hewitt then took over from 'Yoiton' and worked the pump for a couple of years until the Drainage Board put their own man in charge. The electric pump is now automatic with sensors to detect the water levels and turn the pump on and off accordingly.

Left: The derelict Lockgate Mill in about 1960. Supplied by Mike Pickard.

Below: The official opening of the Breydon Electric Pump in 1948.

BURGH CASTLE DRAINAGE MILL

Located on Burgh Castle Marshes near the south wall of Breydon Water at TG489064 there was a drainage windmill. This was a small brick tower mill with common sails driving a small scoop wheel.

A mill was marked on the 1819 Burgh Castle Award Map and on the 1843 Burgh Castle Tithe Map in area 47.

All of these Burgh Castle marshes, and the mill, belonged the Lady of the Manor, Lydia Baret according to both the 1819 Award, and 1843 Tithe Apportionment.

The mill was last worked in the 1890's and pulled down just after the turn of the century. It was not marked on the 1904 OS map. New drainage arrangements were made in the late 1880's whereby all water on these levels was let off into the River Yare at new sluices erected at Southtown Road, Yarmouth.

Later an electric pump house was built sited only a few yards to the east of where the old windmill once stood.

Near to the mill at TG488063 there was a marsh house with outbuildings where the marshman lived. This was shown on the 1819 map and on the 1843 Tithe Map at area 45.

Burgh Castle Drainage Mill from a painting by Charles Harmony Harrison in 1893. Supplied by Peter Allard

PETER ALLARD REMEMBERS BREYDON HOUSEBOATS

A unique feature of Breydon Water for many years was the old houseboats that were dotted around the estuary walls. They were used by wildflowers, naturalists and smelt-fishermen alike and were usually old converted ship's lifeboats or similar vessels, which had outlived their usefulness. All have since disappeared, the last one being unfortunately 'burned' in May 2008.

In my younger days, I can recall half a dozen of them all around the north estuary wall, on the saltings, and one or two situated up the 'north river' towards Acle.

My early bird-watching friend Michael Seago once owned one that was on Duffel's Rond, just the other side of Lockgate Farm. This sadly became a victim of the 1953 floods. Having been so exposed to the full force of the wind and tide, it ended its days on the south wall only to be broken up for firewood. He often related to me the good times he had in it and how it was towed there by Walter Bulldeath, one of the old Breydon wardens.

Top: Peter Allard near Berney Arms in 1963 in his 14 ft gun-punt.
Bottom: Peter Allard at his houseboat near the Breydon 'Dickey Works' in 1964.

So in February 1964, I jumped at the chance of owning a Breydon houseboat. George Rose of High Road, Southtown, one of the last of the Breydon punt gunners had his for sale. It was situated at the extreme western end of the estuary close to the 'Dickey Works' and being so difficult to reach, he was going to sell it and erect another on Duffel's Rond. An agreement was reached at £8 and I bought it with the help of another birding friend, Gordon Morris from Corton. It was in a bit of a state, the hull originally coming from a Norwegian vessel and had laid on Darby's Hard at Gorleston for a number of years before being shipped to Breydon. Having borrowed two old 'car jacks' from Percy Trett, and with the help of Frank Pitts and Phillip Robinson, the whole structure was raised about a foot higher

24

than previously and the bottom completely tarred. The inside was converted and sheets of plywood were transported by punt from North Quay to the far end of the estuary. I can well remember the Coopers lorry arriving with these sheets and me loading them onto the punt and then pulling away from the quayside. I had eight of these sheets some 8 feet by 4 feet slung over the bows of my small 17 foot punt and I had to row this cargo the length of Breydon in a strong easterly gale. By the time I had reached opposite Dufflel's Rond, it had become quite choppy and l had shipped quite a lot of water. On arriving at the houseboat, the punt was virtually full, having being so low at the bows, almost every wave came into the well of the punt. However, all the sheets were used and the inside looked neat and tidy with the small silvery painted 'tortoise' stove at one end and a kitchen at the other end. The outside was painted green and blue and new felt fitted to the roof, Bunks were situated both sides in the main cabin and three small hurricane lamps were purchased for use at night. Everything was transported from Yarmouth by punt, an eight mile row there and back. Paraffin, food and coal for the stove were brought here after a long and sometimes hard row, usually coming up with the tide and going back with it. Once the stove was fired up, it really was cosy and warm and during the summer months, many an hour was spent just watching the boats sail past with the occasional coaster heading to Norwich to photograph. A small transistor radio was useful and I vividly recall listening to the very first transmissions of Radio Caroline during Easter 1964 whilst sitting outside the houseboat. I spent many nights there, sometimes with a friend or two and days were spent bird watching over the marshes and then walking back along the estuary wall via the Berney Arms. Good fry-ups of bacon, beans and sausages were often the order of the early morning and occasional meals were had at the Berney Arms Pub. I even spent one Christmas there much to the annoyance of my parents. One memorable day, I think it was the day after Boxing Day, Dick Foyster and myself having spent the night there, walked over to the Fleet Dyke marshes and flushed no less 52 Short-eared Owls from the vicinity of the old 'Ruined Cottage'. I gave a key to the girl at the Berney Arms Pub, Jane Manning. She often walked past and would call in for a chat. Within a few weeks, Jane had fitted curtains to the windows and the inside had been thoroughly swept and cleaned and all the cups and saucepans were hanging up on hooks. There was not a speck of mud anywhere. One night when sleeping alone, the houseboat started to suddenly shake and on looking nervously outside, I soon discovered a cow had walked onto the rond and was scratching herself on the side of the houseboat. Another frightful night was when I suddenly awoke to find one of the hurricane lamps had caught alight and without a thought, I grabbed it and threw it outside before the whole houseboat was set alight, Had anything gone wrong, the nearest help was several miles away.

Big tides were always a problem however, and often it was difficult to get to the houseboat from the estuary wall without thigh boots. A small cut in the rond allowed a punt to be kept there overnight without damage, Both me and Frank Pitts spent many an hour enlarging this and boarding with planks of wood. However, this small rond was very exposed and was quickly eroding away and keeping out the silt

Left: View of Peter Allard's Houseboat.
Right: the tortoise stove inside the houseboat. Supplied by Peter Allard

mud was a constant problem. Visitors were many and 'Yoiton' Hewitt was a regular, walking the short distance from the pump house when he was in attendance. Michael Seago also came to see me, catching the train from Norwich to Berney Arms and walking the couple miles from the station. I well remember him opening the door of the houseboat to see a Red-necked Grebe swimming past.

For various reasons, I sold the houseboat several years later for £25 to a chap named Coles from Yarmouth who in turn quickly sold it on to a local artist. The top of the houseboat was taken off and it was planned to float it to a rond nearer Yarmouth However, this plan never materialized and by the summer of 1967, the houseboat was a complete wreck. By November 1968, the remains were half covered in mud and soon after, it had been swept away. There is virtually nothing left today except one or two remains of stake posts, but even these are difficult to see. However, I often still stop here and reflect the 'good times' of nearly 50 years ago.

Opposite Page. Top: Mr H Jenner & R Harrison at the houseboat 'Lapwing' in 1936 John Burton Collection. Centre: 'Pintail' 20August 2000. Bottom: 'Whimbrell' 20 August 2000.

DICKEY WORKS

At the western end of Breydon Water, at TG475062 is the remains of the 'Dickey Works'. This is the name given to the old tide jetty or breakwater, constructed for the purpose of deflecting the ebb tide into the deep channel across the estuary towards Yarmouth. Without this, the tide would sweep across the entire width of the estuary.

These Dickey Works are believed to have been built in about 1832. It appears on Emerson's map of 1854, marked 'Tide Jetty', and Booth's map of 1872 shows it clearly marked as the 'Dickey Works'.

With the constant silting up of Breydon Water in the early half of the 19th century, the Great Yarmouth Port and Haven Commissioners were under pressure from users to maintain a navigable passage across the estuary. James Walker, a consultant engineer, was employed in 1826 to advise on the practicability of making Breydon Water navigable for vessels drawing up to ten feet. In 1828 the Commissioners brand new steam dredger began operating at Breydon. The Commissioners were also operating a **'Horse Dydling Engine'**, the eight scoops of which were geared to a whim made to revolve by two horses. It is probable that it was the 'Horse Dydling Engine' which was responsible for building the tide jetty hence the name 'the 'Dickey

Dickey Works A and B on 1880s OS map.

Works', the word 'Dickey' being the old local name for a horse or donkey. Some confirmation of this appears in Arthur Patterson's 'Nature in Eastern Norfolk' of 1905, which states that the 'Dickey Works' were built by a contractor who had a small paddle-boat worked by a donkey -locally known as a 'dickey'! He continues – 'hence the characteristic naming of the construction.'

Another tide jetty at the confluence of the Yare and the Waveney at TG471052, protruding from the tip of the Haddiscoe Island, is also referred to by locals as the 'Dickey Works'. This construction however was built much later in 1864 and like the other construction is in an ineffective and a ruined state.

DAVID HEWITT REMEMBERS

I was born 25 November 1937 at Berney Arms Inn, situated at the Berney Arms Hamlet by the River Yare.

When I was born the Inn was not an Inn, as it is today. It was a marshman's cottage and farm, although it had been an Inn many years previous.

My mother and father Lily and Fred Hewitt were married in the early 1930s and moved into Berney Arms Inn. My father had previously lived at a mill house on the Halvergate Fleet with his parents. My grandfather worked his drainage mill on the Halvergate Fleet and the Breydon Pump.

My sister Robina was born at the Beney Arms Inn.

When living at Berney Arms, my father was a marshman and farmer, and he was also the Berney Arms postman. This post round covered a large area, and as there were no 'roads' across the marshes in the 1930s in the winters it tended to get very muddy so my father used to deliver the mail by horseback; Berney Arms very own 'Pony Express'!

I cannot remember much about living at Berney Arms as my parents moved further up the River Yare to Seven Mile House, Reedham, when I was only five years old. It was while living at Seven Mile House in 1942 my sister Robina and I started school at Reedham. We had to walk about 3 miles each way; this distance was considered nothing in those days. On the way to school we stopped at the railway cottage on Church Road, Reedham, where Eileen and Jack Graves lived, and we carried on going to school, walking along the railway line with the Graves' son and daughter. Their cottage is no longer there.

One of the sad things I remember at Seven Mile House was the collision of two WWII American bomber aircraft on their return from a mission. My father was one of the first at the scene of the crash but nothing could be done, all 21 crew members of the 2 aircraft were killed. During the War hundreds of bombers used to pass over our house day and night, not just American and British but German as well. They used Breydon Water and the River Yare as a navigation aid, on a clear night Breydon Water and the River light up like a beacon. It was watching all the aircraft passing overhead that made me want to join the Royal Air Force, and I joined as a regular in 1955.

My father worked the Oil pump at Seven Mile draining the dykes. I spent hours with my dad in the pump house; it was his pride and joy. We were always cleaning and polishing the pumps, I just loved the noise and smell of the oil pumps.

Just recently in July 2009 I walked along the Wherryman's Way from Reedham to Berney Arms Inn for lunch, passing Seven Mile House: it was the first time I had been back to Seven Mile since I left in 1944. It was nice to see the old oil pump house and it was good to see Polkeys mill restored.

When living at Seven Mile my dad was a marshman and had a small dairy herd and Henry Hewitt (Yoiton) collected our milk by boat and dropped it off at Reedham Quay. My mum used to make fresh butter. She had a separator, which separated the cream of the milk from the whey. The cream and some salt were put in a large butt known as a churn. This butt had a large handle which you turned, and this was known as churning. When it was thick it was taken out of the butt and weighed into one pound blocks and pattered into shape. The whey was fed to the pigs.

Hewitt family members in 1970, supplied by David Hewitt.
From the left: Michael Hewitt, Robina Hewitt, Fred Hewitt, Lily Hewitt, Lily Hewitt and David Hewitt.

During the war in the early 1940s when food was in short supply, my dad would go to Great Yarmouth about twice a week by horse and cart and take butter, eggs and various vegetables, especially field mushrooms which were plentiful on the marshes in those days. He would barter his goods for other items of food or other goods he required.

During the 1930s there were about 50 houses scattered over the marshes close to the vicinity of the River Yare. There was a real sense of friendship and comrardre between the marshmen and if one person needed help all the others would rally to help with no fee or favour ever asked in return.

In April 1944, when I was seven, we left Seven Mile House and moved to what was known as 'Nowhere Farm' situated in the Bure loop near Gt. Yarmouth. The address was later changed to White House Farm, Runham Vauxhall. When we moved we moved by wherry, I think the wherryman's name was Mr Gedge.

PEGGY SAWBRIDGE REMEMBERS

My family and I had many happy boating holidays on the Norfolk Broads. My father had a long sailing tradition, as his uncle, with four daughters only, had been hiring wherries since the late 1800s, (there being then no alternatives) and my father would be invited to join them. All the work would be done by the two crewmen, but Jack, as my father was then known, picked up all the information he could, which came in very useful later.

Langley Detached Drainage Mill in 1934.
Supplied by Peggy Sawbridge.

As time went by, Jack was twice married. By his first wife he had, among others, John and Lucy who figure in these pages. After her death and a decent interval he married my mother, and Beth and I resulted. Our first attempt at a boating holiday was in a sailing cruiser, but for assorted reasons this was unsuccessful, so the following year in 1934 we hired from Jack Powles a large cruiser called 'Silver Foam'. I was by then twelve and Beth was seven and I kept a diary of the voyage, from which the following is an extract which I dedicate to Beth who always made us smile whether in or out of the water:

'... I woke up at 6:45. We got up and went to fetch the milk. We then had breakfast and started at about 9:30. We stopped to get petrol and further on we saw a bittern. We went through Yarmouth and the bridge leading to Breydon Water was open, and we saw it shut. We crossed Breydon and moored on the Yare for dinner. A farmer, whose name was Mr Hewitt, told us that we were stuck on posts, and so we were! We had to wait till midnight. I felt ill all the afternoon, and slept in Beth's bunk. Mummy came at twelve, because Beth was frightened of the rocking. The farmer came and helped Daddy and John, but it was a long time before we could get off and we only just managed it.

Beth was still frightened, so Mummy came and slept in the double bunk with her, while Mary went to sleep with Lucy. Poor Beth was sick, but soon after we all went

31

to sleep, having just reached our new mooring place, where we were to spend the rest of the night. I woke again at 2:45, and was sick, soon afterwards Mummy was sick too'.

     ... Next day we headed for Reedham and there we saw the Reedham Swing Bridge open, and a big ship called 'Acrity' pass through. Many other ships followed it. I went out of the boat for a while. Once we all got back on the boat we went up to Norwich but were not allowed to moor there, so we went back to Whitlingham for lunch. After lunch we watched a dredger at work.'

Following the incident at Berney Arms, my father, the Rev. John E. B. Sawbridge, wrote to the County Council, the only relevant authority then, and told them that 'Unsafe to Moor' notices should be put up in any other similar places throughout the Broads Network. In subsequent years such notices were used.

Motor Cruiser 'Sparkling Foam' at Reedham in 1936 . Supplied by Peggy Sawbridge.

Vessel stuck in the ice near Berney Arms in 1929. Supplied by John Baker.

'Resolute' on Breydon Water in the early 1950s by David Pyett. The Resolute was used between Gorleston and Great Yarmouth for many years but after WWII she ran broads trips usually from Yarmouth along the Waveney, until she was sold in about 1967 to the Veteran Steamship Society.

The houseboat 'Greylag' on the rond near the Berney Arms Inn. Ron, Jack and Bob Carter and friends used the houseboat as their base from which they could go 'babbing' for eels. Supplied by Ron Carter.

Stanley Hewitt in 1959 from Edward Roberts. Stanley was the last marshman to live at RavenHall and the last marshman at Ashtree Farm, Beney Arms.

MR FREDERICK SAMUEL BAKER wrote about Colman's River transport to Norwich:

'Colman's Wharf was a transhipment base and storage depot, the next process was keeping the Mills at Carrow supplied with the raw materials they needed. For this purpose in my early days a fleet of wherries was employed.

......In 1901the steam tug **Kestral** was purchased and thereafter the wherries were towed both ways. The Kestral besides being a tug also carried about 90 tons of cargo. She was sold in 1924 to a Thames lighterage company and so returned to the scene of her former activities, the River Thames.

The Kestral was replaced by the **Mustard Pot**, built at Goole and brought by sea to Yarmouth. This new Tug carried no cargo being designed for towing purposes only, and was very powerfully built. When the River Yare was icebound in Reedham in February 1929, and the Coasters were held fast in the ice, it was the Mustard Pot which cut a lane through the ice floes and released the vessels so they could proceed to Yarmouth on their journey seawards. The tug became well known to all users of the River in view of the fact that she carried on either side of her funnel two large brass replicas of her name. In the early part of the last War she was requisitioned by the Admiralty and finally purchased by the government.

Some members of the Baker family onboard the Mustard Pot.
Supplied by John Baker.

Prior to the advent of the Mustard Pot, the wherries mentioned previously had been replaced by lighters or dumb barges with a carrying capacity of 120 tons. There were six of these all named after birds, and with the exception of the first, which came from the Thames, were all built at Yarmouth. They were kept fully employed for more than 40 years.

The 'Mustard Pot' at Carrow, Norwich in 1925, from Peter Allard Collection.

Colman's Berth at Great Yarmouth in the 1920s from John Baker.

An additional water transport activity was the weekly service of a coasting steamer supplying the London wharf with manufactured goods brought down river by lighter and transhipped at Yarmouth. The first vessel chartered for the purpose in 1902 was the S. S. Jeanie Hope, followed by the Pearl, Peronne, Yellowhammer and Norwich Trader. The coasting service was continued though both Word Wars in spite of the difficulties and dangers encountered, and came to an end in October 1945. ...'

Langley Detached Mill in 1959 by Edward Roberts.

RAVEN HALL, Langley Detached Parish   TG466045

Raven Hall stands on Langley Detached Marshes on the Island by the river Yare and opposite Berney Arms. It is thought to have been built in the seventeenth century.

A building is marked on Faden's map of 1797 at this location although it is not named. On Bryant's map of 1826 it is shown as **5 Mile House** and on later Ordnance Survey maps as Raven Hall. It is also sometimes referred to as Ravens Hall.

It is built of bricks and has a thatched roof. It was last re-thatched in 1995 and a new chimney was put on at the same time. It is a grade II listed building.

Some past occupant include the Gowen family who were listed in the 1841 to 1871 census returns, the Thaxter family, listed in the 1871 to 1891 censuses and the Hewitt family from 1901 census till about 1962. All were marsh farmers and were responsible for the nearby drainage mill.

The Langley detached marshes and Raven Hall were owned by the Beauchamp-Proctor family for many years, and became part of the Dashwood estate until in 1961 when it became the property of Mr Askew.

In 1969 Raven Hall was bought by a Mr and Mrs Len & Aase Williams as a holiday home. In the early 1990s they sold the house to Mr and Mrs Browne-Wilkinson who used the place as a holiday home.

LANGLEY DETACHED DRAINAGE MILL.

This is located in Langley Detached Parish on the Haddiscoe Island, TG465044.

Langley Mill, sometimes called the **Red mill**, or **Hewitt's Mill** stands close to Raven Hall. It was shown on the 1797 map as a drainage windmill but un-named. It is shown on all subsequent maps. The earliest mill was probably a cloth-sailed mill.

The current mill was probably rebuilt at some time, probably sometime between 1840 and 1880, and was a redbrick tower, patent sail mill of medium height, with three storeys, excluding the cap. It was about thirty feet to the curb, with two doors and one window. The walls at the base were about 2 foot thick, and about 18 inches thick at the top.

When working it had four patent sails each with 9 double bays and three shutters per bay, giving 54 shutters per sail. The sails turned anticlockwise.

The cap was a white boat-shaped cap, which after conversion to a holiday home was painted red, and the fantail had eight vanes. The mill drove an external scoopwheel with a diameter about 18 feet, and with paddles about 10 inches across, and the hood was painted white. It drained about 200 acres at the tip of the Island.

The windmill continued to function until about 1941/2 when the fantail was blown off. Isaac Hewitt of Reedham dismantled the sails and a portable steam engine was then brought in and used to drive the scoopwheel using a belt. The steam engine was used for a couple of years until the boiler blew up.

In the late 1940's and early 1950's an International tractor engine was connected to the scoopwheel and used to pump these marshes.

The derelict mill was part of the Beauchamp estate and was bought in about 1948 by Mr Roy Clark for about £25 and converted into a holiday home. A bungalow extension was added. The mill was later sold to a Mr Laurence H. Davis, in about 1959, and then in about 1971 to Mr and Mrs Mackley. Mains electricity was laid on here at the same time as it was at Ravenhall. Mr I.G. Ingram, bought the mill in about 1981. Water is now plumbed in from a borehole and he has also installed a septic tank. The mill is listed as a grade II building. Some repair work was started in September 2001 with the aid of a grant from South Norfolk Council, and a new cap was constructed, the millwright was a Mr Neil Metcalf from Lincolnshire. The present owner is Daniel Webster and the mill is used as a holiday let.

The Berney Arms Inn in the early 1950s by David Pyett.

'Golden Galleon' in 1955 at Berney Arms.

View from the top of Berney Arms mill in the early 1950s showing the bungalow, cottages and the inn in the distance. Photographs by David Pyett

Thomas J. Metcalf's cargo boats 'Jim M' and 'Polly M' photographed from the Langley Detached Mill with Berney Arms Mill in the background circa 1948. Supplied by Rod Clarke. 'Jim M 'was built in 1944 with a gross tonnage of 410, 'Polly M' was built in 1937 with a gross tonnage of 360.

BERNEY ARMS INN (TG468052)

The inn was probably built in the eighteenth century although it was not marked on Faden's map of 1797. It does appear on all subsequent maps. It was a public house until 1909 when it lost it's licence and became a farmhouse. By about 1943 the building was in a bad state of repair and was left vacant for a few years. The Inn belonged to the Berney family estate until they sold it in about 1947 to Aubrey Appleton and Denis Robertson. After a time they sold it to Mr Matthews who repaired the pub and put on a new roof.

Chris Sheppard in 2003. Landlord at the Berney Arms

The owner at the time of the Reedham Tithe Apportionment circa 1840 was Thomas Trench Berney.

View of the side of the old Berney Arms in 1949 from R. Mathews.

The pub was an alehouse and was leased by the brewery Steward & Patterson in about 1875. When it eventually regained its licence it became a freehouse. It was referred to as 'The Old Inn' when it reopened but the name was changed back to **Berney Arms** on 12 February 1962.

Some occupants of the Berney Arms Inn:

Date	License / Occupier	Description / Notes
1821	Thomas Riches	Publican
1826&1830	James Barrett	Publican
1836	John Cater	Victualler
c.1840	William George	'Occupier', but did not live here.
1841 & 1845	Robert Rushmer	Victualler
1851	Horace Gillbert	Innkeeper
1861	James Knights	Innkeeper
1864	Charles Knights	Victualler / a brother to James and did not live on premises.
1868	Charles Knights	Victualler
1871	James Knights	Innkeeper
08.03 1875	Charles Carver	Innkeeper
25.11.1878	Walter Daniels	Victualler & Farmer
15.11.1886	Frederick Carter	Victualler
29.09.1890	Robert Thaxter	Publican
10.07.1899	John Andrew	Victualler
20.08.1900	John Andrew	Licence reduced to 6 days
20.06.1909	John Andrew	Pub lost licence. Licence set to expire on 7 June 1910.
1910	Thomas & Eliza Hewitt & family	They used 'the old inn' as a farmhouse.
c.1933	Mr Cafferoy (?) & family	Kept goats inside.
c.1937 to 1942	Fred & Lilly Hewitt & family	Fred worked Breydon Pump
c.1943	Vacant	Roof needing repair.
c.1947	Aubrey Appleton & Dennis Robertson	Bought the old inn from the Berney family.
c.1949	Reginald & Elsie Matthews	He renovated the buildings in 1950 and turned it into a guesthouse.
c.1952	Dick & Muriel Foster	
1953	Dick Forster	Club Licence obtained
1954 to 1960	Charles L. Schofield	Pub Off Licence was renewed in Feb. 1955 and full licence in 1960.
26.09.1960	William Kendall Barnes	
13.06.1966	Robert Leslie Manning	
1974		Briefly owned by Northampton Brewery
c.1974 to 2000	Robert McLaughlan	
2000	Chris Sheppard & Carole Harvey	Tenants. Pub owned by Tapestry Taverns.
2007-Present	John & Tracy	Tenants. "

BERNEY ARMS HIGH MILL (TG465049)

Faden's map 1797 shows a 'Drainage' mill at this approximate location. This was probably a cloth-sailed mill.

Berney Arms High Mill. Left: In full working order in the 1930s The building on the left is part of the remains of the old cement works buildings.
Right: The mill after repair by the Ministry of Works in the late 1950s.

The Norfolk Chronicle 10th Feb 1821 mentions a windmill as part of the Reedhan Cement / Brickworks at Berney Arms so the mill then must be assumed to be grinding the cement clinker. We cannot be certain if it was also draining the marshes. It is quite probable that the cloth-sail windmill had been replaced by a Patent sail windmill by then.

The Norfolk Chronicle 20th April 1822 also mentions that a Steam Engine is now part of the cement works. This Steam Engine presumably was built in 1821 as it was not mentioned in February of 1821. Bryant's map of 1826 shows a Windmill and a Steam Engine next to Kilns.

The Norfolk Chronicle 13th September 1828 mentions a Patent Sail Windmill capable of driving 4 pairs of stones but used for driving circular saws along with a 10hp Steam Engine. The Norfolk Chronicle 25th June 1836 mentions again both a Patent Sail Windmill and a 10 hp Steam Engine employed for Sawing,

Grinding cement and Draining the marshes. (It is not clear if the windmill or the Steam Engine or both are used for the marsh drainage but it is probable that both were used for all three jobs.)

The Reedham Tithe Apportionment map circa 1840 mentions 'Factory, Mill and Yards' but does not give details of the mill, and the Norfolk Chronicle 1847 mentions a 5 Storey Patent Sail Windmill capable of driving 4 pairs of stones along with a 12hp Steam Engine.

Millwrights from the firm of R. Thompson of Alford in Lincolnshire attaching the sails to the Berney Arms Mill on 23 May 2007.

The Norfolk Chronicle 1860 mentions a 24hp Brick Tower Patent Sail Windmill and a 12 hp Steam Engine both used in the Cement Trade.

The Ordnance Survey map of 1883 shows a Pumping Windmill for draining the marshes and a disused Cement factory. Perhaps the Steam Engine is part of the disused facilities. The mill standing today is seven storeys high and, is said to have been built around 1865 by Edward Stolworthy. Whether this was a completely new build, a part rebuild job or simply a hain is not known.

It is believed that Barnes was the millwright who in about 1883 converted the mill to be used for drainage only. The present Berney Arms High Mill is a tarred brick tower mill with an iron stage on the third floor. It is seven floors and stands 70 feet high with an external diameter of 28 feet at ground level and has a boat shaped cap. At the time of writing the mill is undergoing restoration work and is without sails and fantail but it has 4 sails, an 8-bladed fantail, an iron gallery, and a chain pole. The 4 sails were double-shuttered and the span is roughly 80 feet. According to Rex Wailes the sails were not identical, one pair having come from another mill. The scoop wheel, which was used for draining the marshes is 24 feet in diameter and stands separate from the mill. It is encased in a narrow brick-lined culvert and covered with a wooden hoodway. The paddles are eleven inches wide.

After 1883 it was used only as a drainage mill, and would have been worked by the marshmen William Hewitt, (' King Billy'), Jimmy Hewitt, ('Wesmacot') and Henry Hewitt, ('Yoiton'), until 1949 when it was replaced by the electric pump.

The redundant mill was taken over by the Ministry of Public Buildings and Works in 1951 and is now owned by English Heritage.

The mill was opened to the public in May 1956. During the winter of 1961/2 the mill suffered damage to the sails, fantail and gallery and following this a full restoration was started in 1965 and completed in July 1967. These repairs were carried out by Smithdale and Sons. The mill was overhauled again in 1972/3 and re-tarred and repainted. The sails were removed in 1999 and the cap of the mill was removed 4th November 2002, repaired, and replaced 6th May 2003. The tower was re-tarred and doors and windows repaired during the summer of 2003, and the sails were eventually replaced in May 2007.

REEDHAM CEMENT WORKS AT BERNEY ARMS

The following is from NRO/STA518:

In 1843 T.T. Berney leased the cement works, including the windmill, and 3 cottages to John Cutler Ramsden and Charles Stephenson Ramsden at an annual rent of £200, to be paid quarterly. (Note: The Ramsdens lived in Hamburgh in Germany.)

In March 1847, after Ramsden & Co quit the works, T.T. Berney had a Mr Ollett assess the repairs required to be done to the Cement Works. Ollett's estimate for general repairs was £129 – 0 – 9.5d. Berney wanted the Ramsdens to pay for these repairs.

Ramsden's solicitor, C. Cory, in April 1847 sent a letter to Berney to say that his clients wished to claim back their £75 deposit which was paid when they took out the lease, and also claimed £100 for 4 years drainage of 160 acres at 2/6d per acre.

A letter from STOLWORTHY dated 11th July 1857: *'Having been over the cement works to look at the grinding stones to mill and engine I am of opinion they are worth about thirty five pounds. Those in the mill not being French Burr are not worth more than Eleven pounds when new'*

A letter from STOLWORTHY dated 2nd July 1858: *'The irons, brasses and Bridging Pot used belonging to the stones removed from the windmill could be replaced for the sum of £4 – 10 – 0d.'*

In June 1857 a draft agreement between T. T. Berney and WILLIAM COLLET REYNOLDS was prepared for Reynolds to lease the cement works from June 24th at a rent of £50. A latter document in 1858 gave Reynolds the option of taking the lease for 14 years from 24th June 1858 at a rent of £200 / year, but Reynolds only took on the lease for a year and in 1859 finished leasing the works. After Reynolds quit the cement works in 1859 James Nesbitt ran the works on Berney's behalf, and Nesbitt and Berney continued to try to find someone to lease the works.

Tucks Mill at Berney Arms. Peter Allard.

A letter dated 29 Nov 1864 on blue company paper, with a printed header *'Berney Arms Portland Cement Works, Burgh Castle, Gt. Yarmouth'*, and signed by James Nesbit, says among other things, that the rent would be £300/year and included 5 cottages and a Foreman's cottage, there is a steam engine, there is 3 pair of 4ft 9ins diameter stones, a windmill to drain the marshes, and that he has loaded vessels of 130 tons alongside the works.

In Dec 1864 a letter was sent back reporting that de Castro's clients 'cannot lease it at the price and they are trying to form a company'.

ASH TREE FARM (Berney Arms at TG464048)

The farmhouse is believed to have been built in 1750-52. It is marked on Faden's map of 1797 and called 'Five mile House'. It is also marked on Wyand's map of 1823, and on the Reedham Tithe Map of circa 1840, where it was shown as area 34, occupied by James Duffield and owned by Thomas Trench Berney. It is also shown on all of the Ordnance Survey Maps since 1883 to the present time as 'Ash Tree Farm'.

TUCKS MILL. (TG461044 Berney Arms)

This was a drainage mill and though not marked on Faden's Map of 1797 it did appear on Wyand's Map of 1823, suggesting it was built sometime in the early 1800's. On Bryant's Map of 1826, it was labelled as 'Berney's Mill'.

On the Reedham Tithe Apportionment map, circa 1840, it is marked in area 53 as 'Mill, Yards and Rand' and was owned by the Reedham Lord of the Manor John Francis Leathes and 'occupied' by a Thomas Sibel. The mill was also shown on Ordnance Survey Maps of 1884, and 1926 where it was shown as a drainage windpump. It is probable that it may have been rebuilt at some stage in the late nineteenth century.

The last mill was a brick tower mill of average height and tarred. It carried four patent sails, which turned anti-clockwise into the wind. These were double shuttered with 9 bays, with 3 shutters in each bay and a total of 54 shutters per sail. The mill had a boat-shaped cap with no gallery and carried an 8-bladed fantail. The sails were adjusted with a chain guide pole with a Y-wheel. It drove a large scoop wheel. Within living memory, this mill has always been known as Tuck's Mill.

Tuck's mill was the responsibility of Mr Fred Burgess of Seven Mile House in the 1930's, and he employed Jack Farrow, who lived at No.1 Cottage, Berney Arms to operate the drainage mill.

On 26th April 1941 the sails were caught by the wind from behind and because the brake had not been fully applied they began to turn backwards. The friction started a fire destroying the cap and the sails. The brick shell stood for several years until about 1950 when Reginald Matthews who owned the Berney Inn at the time bought the shell for £100 from Stimpson. He employed someone to dismantle the tower brick by brick, and used the bricks to build a septic tank at the inn and make other repairs to the inn.

SIX MILE MILL,

Located on the Island in Chedgrave detached Parish at **TG452034**.
The mill was shown as a drain mill on Faden's map but not named, and shown on Bryant's map as **'Chedgrave Mill'**. It was also shown on the Chedgrave Tithe Apportionment map of 1839, and it was marked on all O.S. maps as a draining pump.

It was also known as Hewitt's Mill as it was worked by Stephen Hewitt, and before him by his father William Hewitt, 'King Billy', and his grandfather Edward Hewitt.

The original mill is thought to have been built in the 18th century, and was probably rebuilt around 1870. The tarred redbrick tower was about 21 ft 8 inches to the curb and it had an internal fireplace and a flue on the east wall. It was three storeys high, including the cap floor, and had two doors. Above each door there was a window, one of which was bricked in at sometime. The walls are about two feet thick and the tower diameter was about 14 feet.

It was a cloth sailed mill winded by a tailpole. The sails turned anticlockwise into the wind. It drove an external scoopwheel about 14 feet diameter, the wooden scoopwheel hood was painted black, and the boat-shaped wooden cap on

Six-Mile Mill on the Haddiscoe Island on 17th September 2006.

top of the tower was painted white. It drained about 500 acres.

The windmill was last worked in about 1946. A diesel engine was then used for a year or two to drive the scoopwheel, and after 1948 a Standard tractor was used for driving the scoopwheel.

After the 1953 flood a diesel engine was brought in and used to drive the old scoopwheel. An Admiralty pump with a one foot bore was also used. This pump used 4 gallons of fuel an hour and was filled up every two hours. Before the marshes were drained the pump had used 11,000 gallons of fuel having been used continuously day and night for seven weeks.

The tower still stands and is derelict. It is listed as a Grade II building by Norfolk County Council and is cared for by the Norfolk Windmills Trust.

SIX-MILE HOUSE, stood near the mill at TG453034. This was marked on Faden's Map of 1797, Bryant's Map of 1826, the Tithe Map of 1839 and on the OS maps and named as Six Mile House on them all. It is sometimes referred to by locals as Burnt House, because the house burned down on 26th September 1926. A spark came from the wash-house chimney pot went onto the thatched roof and started the fire.

UPPER SEVEN MILE MILL on the Island in Chedgrave Detached Parish, was shown on Faden's map next to Upper Seven Mile house at about TG446025 but was not shown on any later maps. No other information is available but it was probably a cloth-sailed mill.

SEVEN-MILE REEDHAM

This area, which is about seven miles along the river Yare from Great Yarmouth, is an interesting area, which has been the home of three windmills, two steam pumps, a diesel pump and an electric pump, all of which were used for draining the marshes. There were also two dwellings here, Seven-Mile House, which still stands next to the river, and another cottage near to Polkey's mill.

CADGE'S MILL (TG446036) Reedham.

This was known as Cadge's or Kedge's Mill, but the origin of the name is not known. It has also been called 'Batchies Mill' and 'Stimpsons Mill'. It was marked on Faden's, Wyand's and Bryant's map as a drainage mill, though not named, but it is not clear from the Tithe Apportionment if a mill was here around 1840. The land where the mill stands, was owned by the Rev William John Emmitt at the time of the Tithe Apportionment. The Norwich Mercury 6 July 1867: *'Auction 690a 3r 16p with Marsh House, Stable, Cow House & other buildings and Drainage Mill.... Trustees of the late Rev W. J. Emmett'*

The current mill was probably built about 1880. It has been suggested that when it was first built it had buckets attached to the scoopwheel, but that this was not very successful. The scoopwheel was inside the mill. This was a 4 storey high tarred brick tower mill with two doors, patent sails, an 8 bladed fantail and a typical boat shaped cap. The scoopwheel was sixteen feet in diameter and the paddles 14 inches wide. It was last worked in about 1941. This mill had a fireplace inside for preventing the internal water lane from freezing up in severe weather.

The controls, switchgear and transformer for the new electric pump were installed in this mill in the early 1980's, and a flat corrugated roof was fitted.

STEAM PUMP (TG446035) Reedham.

This was built in about 1880, and has the inscription 'J.W.R. 1880'. This refers to John William Rose of Reedham Hall, who was listed as Lord of the Manor of Reedham in the 1883 directory and who owned many of the marshes near to Thaxter's marsh house and Polkey's mill. It may have been built to replace an earlier steam drainage mill at TG447036, or simply as an aid for the adjacent Polkey's mill. It was last worked in about 1941 when the diesel plant took over.

The building is constructed of brick, with cast iron window frames and the roof is corrugated iron sheeting. The interior walls of the building were covered in pine panelling and the floors were black and white tiles.

The engine was a single cylinder horizontal engine with a 12-inch bore and 24 inch stroke. It was fitted with Meyer expansion gear and produced about 75 horsepower. This drove a turbine pump through 'double bevel gears' and a countershaft. The engine was built by Richard Barnes, a millwright of Great Yarmouth. The lift of water from dyke to river was about 5 to 7 feet.

The pump was probably operated by either the Thaxter family or the Burgess family who lived in the adjacent marsh houses. A Mr Bob Burgess is believed to have been one of the last men to operate the steam pump.

Much of the machinery of the old mill was sold in the 1960's as scrap metal.

The tall chimneystack blew down in 1976 during the winter gales, but most of the buildings of this old steam mill are still in existence. Under the 'Land of the Windmills' project driven by the Norfolk Windmills Trust and the Broads Authority, and funded by the Broadland District Council, a Heritage Lottery grant and a grant from WREN (Waste recycling environmental body), this engine house was repaired in 2006.

POLKEY'S MILL (TG445035)

This mill was marked on Faden's map of 1797 and on all subsequent maps. It has also been known as 'Seven Mile Mill' and 'South Mill' and the current name is thought to be after a marshman 'Polkey' Thaxter who worked the mill for many years. The present mill was probably built between 1840 and 1880. It drove a scoopwheel and on the floodgate it has inscribed 'Barnes'. This probably refers to Richard Barnes, a millwright of Southtown, Great Yarmouth who was active in the 1860's through to the early 1880's.

Seven Mile Reedham 17th September 2006. Polkey's Mill on the left and Cadges Mill on the right. The diesel pump and the steam pump house are in the centre.

It was a black, tarred brick tower mill of medium height, which had patent sails, an eight-bladed fantail and a boat-shaped cap. The mill last worked in about 1941. Ivan Mace remembers a chef from a pub had the mill in the early 1960's but he didn't like the coypus and left the area. Most of the machinery remains inside the mill. A temporary aluminium cap, fitted in about 1980, and the remains of the sails were still attached until recently when restoration work began. The sails were removed 26th March 2003. Restoration by Vincent Pargetter was completed in 2005.

NORTH MILL (TG443036) Reedham.

This was not shown on Faden's, Wyand's, or Bryant's maps and first appears on the O.S. map of 1837, and then on the Tithe Map circa 1840. It was probably built sometime between about 1825 and 1836, and was probably built as a 'helper' mill to assist the water from the Seven Mile Levels to Polkey's mill alongside the river. The mill and nearby marshes were owned by John Francis Leathes at the time of the Tithe Apportionment and was occupied by Mary Jary a farmer in Reedham. The mill was a small tower mill, 3 storeys high and had two doors and a window at the first floor. It was about ten feet in diameter at the ground with walls about twenty inches thick and the brickwork is about 23 feet high. It drove a scoop-wheel and was probably last used before 1900.

In a 'Schedule of lands drained by the Reedham Hall Mill', NRO/MC165/6/2, circa 1848, Polkey's Mill and the North Mill together drained 798a 3r 14p.

DIESEL PUMP (TG447036)

This was built in 1941 and had 3 single cylinder Ruston and Hornsby engines supplied new in 1941 by William Foster & Co. Lincolnshire. It has a concrete floor and 3 foot walls supporting steel framing clad with corrugated sheet metal, painted green. Two engines power the centrifugal pumps marked Gwynnes, and the other, a starting engine with 2 flywheels, drives a Ruston and Hornsby air compressor and a suction priming pump. Outside is a cistern holding cooling water and a tank for holding diesel fuel. Fuel was delivered by boat. It was last used in the early 1980's and was superseded by an electric pump. After the 1953 floods Reggie Mace had this pump working continuously for 3 days. It is now in the care of The Norfolk Windmills Trust and is still functional. The diesel pump was moved closer to Polkeys Mill when the alterations to the river wall were made in recent years.

STEAM PUMP (TG447036) Reedham.

This lay to the east of the diesel pump. It was not marked on any of the early maps (ie Faden's, Wyand's, Bryant's or the Reedham Tithe map) and so was probably built around 1840/50, perhaps to drain the marshes and replace the early Cadge's windmill . It was probably last used in the 1880's. The land where it was built was, at the time of the Tithe Apportionment, circa 1840, owned by the Rev William John Emmitt.

MR SYDNEY HOWLETT REMEMBERS.

When I attended Reedham School our Teacher Miss Mount gave us a project of recording the ships which went up the River Yare. Miss Mount was in touch with the port authorities to get information about the ships and their cargoes.

Extracts from my project book of 1939 are as follows:

Date	Name of Vessel	From	Cargo	To
21 April	River Witham	Keadby	Coal	Thos. May Ltd
" .	River Trent	Blyth	Coal	R. Coller & Sons
22 April	David M	Blyth	Coal	Thorpe Power Stn
"	Ethel Everard	London	Grain	Reckitt & Colman
"	Boston Trader	Rotterdam	Grain	R.J.Read Ltd
23 April	Sagacity	Blyth	Coal	Thorpe Power Stn
" .	Viking	Port Talbot	Tin plate	Reckitt & Colman
24 April	Marie May	London	Cement	Lacey & Lincoln Ltd
26 April	Norwich Trader	Newcastle	Coal	Thorpe Power Stn
"	Adaptity	Antwerp	Grain	R.J.Read
27 April	David M	Blyth	Coal	Thorpe Power Stan
5 May	Accruity	Blyth	Coal	Thorpe Power Stn
6 May	Adapity	Blyth	Coal	Thorpe Power Stn
7 May	Norwich Trader	Antwerp	Grain	R.J.Read
"	River Trent	Keadby	Coal	R.Coller & Sons
"	Assurity	Barton	Tiles	R.R.Ruymp & Sons
"	Charles M	Blyth	Coal	Thorpe Power Stn
8 May	River Witham	Keadby	Coal	Thos Moy Ltd
"	Gold Bell	Keadby	Coal	Norwich C.W.S.
9 May	Accruity	Blyth	Coal	Thorpe Power Stn
10 May	Lady Maud	London	Grain	Reckitt & Colman
11 May	Norwich Trader	Antwerp	Grain	R.J.Read
11 May	Greenhithe	London	Rice	Reckitt & Colman
12 May	Charles M	Blyth	Coal	Thorpe Power Stn
"	Amenity	Blyth	Coal	Thorpe Power Stn
25 May	Thomas M	Blyth	Coal	Thorpe Power Stn
26 May	Sedulity	Blyth	Coal	Thorpe Power Stn
27 May	Charles M	Blyth	Coal	Thorpe Power Stn
"	Signality	Blyth	Coal	Thorpe Power Stn
29 May	Ability	Goole	Coal	Thomas Moy Ltd
"	River Trent	Blyth	Coal	R. Coller & Sons
30 May	Robrix	Pontrieux	Grain	R.J. Read
31 May	Aseity	Blyth	Coal	Thorpe Power Stn
"	Polly M	Blyth	Coal	Thorpe Power Stn

Information from the River Yare Commission sent by Mr Davidson, Collector of River Tolls at Carrow Bridge to 24th March 1939:

Craft:

735 seagoing cargo vessels entered the Yare at Yarmouth bound for Cantley and Norwich

21 seagoing cargo vessels entered the Yare at Yarmouth, diverting at Reedham via the Cut for the Waveney.

Pleasure Craft:

Approximately   350 motor craft
                           130 Sailing craft
                           200 rowing boats
                           50 house boats.

Cargoes:

The following were the principal cargoes carried on this river for the year ending 24th March 1939:

Cargo	Tons
Cement	6,438
Coal	204,299
General (groceries)	15,722
Flour	2,074
Grain	135,588 qrs
Molasses	6,653
Petrol	9,747
Rice	6,436
Scrap Iron	7,402
Spelter	975
Sugar	18,365
Tiles & Bricks	1,974,200
Wood	22,062 loads
Wood Pulp Boards	3,437

REEDHAM DETACHED MILL.

Located at TG429014 on the south bank of the river in Reedham Detached Parish on the Haddiscoe Island, in the area once called 'Hall Meadows'.

This was shown on Faden's map as a' Drain W. Mill' and on Bryant's map of 1826 as 'Reedham Mill'. The mill and Yard were marked on the 1840 Tithe Map and owned and occupied by John Stracey. On the 1823 Wyands map the marshes were occupied by John Benns and owned by T.T. Berney. There was no marshman's cottage here and the John Benns occupying the land in 1823 was probably the John Benns who lived in the farmhouse next to the Raveningham Detached Pump. This early mill was probably a cloth-sail mill.

RAVENINGHAM DETACHED (No 2) MILL AND PUMP.

Located at TG426013 on the South bank of the Yare near Reedham. This area is now part of Norton Subcourse civil parish and the pump is often referred to as the **Norton Steam Mill** or the **Benns Steam pump.**

Two drainage mills were shown near here on Faden's map, marked as 'Norton Drain Mills'. Bryant's map of 1823 also shows a mill near here, marked as 'Raveningham Mill'. It is probable that the mills then were cloth-sailed windmills.

The 1841 Tithe Apportionment for Raveningham, with the map drawn in 1839 gives the owner and occupier of the mill at this location as John Benns. The mill was by then a steam pump. The steam engine originally drove a scoopwheel, and later, the scoopwheel was replaced by a turbine. It has been suggested that the original configuration was a Cornish boiler and a beam or grasshopper engine driving a scoopwheel of about 15 foot diameter. These were believed to have been replaced by a Galloway engine in about 1848. The Benns family lived in the nearby farmhouse, and in the 1861 and 1871 censuses a John Benns is listed as an engine man rather than as a marshman or marsh labourer, clearly indicating that the pump was a steam-pump. The steam pump continued to work until the 1930's and was eventually replaced by an electric pump. Much of the buildings were gone before the 1950's but the chimney remained till it was pulled down in about 1964.

THE SHIP INN

This is located on the riverside near to the Reedham Swing Bridge. The Inn was **not** marked on the 1825 map. The first reference to the Ship Inn appears in the 1836 directory, which lists a William Shepherd as a victualler and coal-dealer. The first of the Inn buildings must have been built, therefore, sometime between 1825 and 1836.

The Ship probably began as a beer house and was a Freehouse but in the early 1900's it became a tied house to the wine merchants & brewers 'Diver & Son' of Gt. Yarmouth. It was later a Charrington's House but is once again now a Freehouse and privately owned.

Date	Licensee / Occupant	Notes/ SHIP INN
1836	William Shepherd	Victualler & Coal-dealer. **Ship**
1839	Hannah Shepherd	
1841	William Case	Innkeeper, age 35.
1854	William Stockings	Innkeeper
1857	James Benns	Publican (Place not specified)
1861	Richard Mutten	Age 28. His wife is Mary, age 27, and their son is Charles age 4 months.
1875	Mrs Mary Mutten	
1881	Charles Jacob Mutten	Licensed Victualer, age 21. (He was a son of Richard & Mary). His wife is Emily A. Mutten, age 23. 1890: Boat builder, boat owner & coal dealer. 1900:Wherry Owner, Brickmaker, Coal Merchant, Wind Miller, Farmer and The Ship Public House.
11.11.1901	Emily Anna Mutten	The Ship Public House. Wherry Owner, Brickmaker, Coal Merchant & Farmer in 1904.
02.07.1906	Henry Jacob Carter	.
14.07.1910	Walter William Gooderham	
22.05.1916	Ellen Pricilla Gooderham	
17.05.1920	James Albert Heath	
25.08.1930	Edith Heath	
09.02.1931	Alfred Perry	
30.09.1935	George Walter Everitt	
26.04.1937	Frank Hudson	
12.02.1940	John Berry Lawrence	
21.09.1942	Frank Sidney Clover	
10.11.1947	Frederick Stanley Chatters	
13.03.1950	William Cross	
01.10.1956	Edward William Ewles	
02.11.1964	William Ernest Dickens	
1973	Terry Billings	
1979	Roy Cavanagh	
1981	Graham & Jackie Carlton	
1989 - Present	Graham Carlton & Peter Clutton	

Top: 1953 View of Reedham riverside looking west from the Holly Farm Road bridge showing the rear of the Reedham Ship public house on the left. The building in the centre was once the Brickmaker's Arms Public house.

Bottom: View from Maypole Hill Reedham looking south-east towards the New Cut. The New Cut joins the Yare at about TG427014. The Haddiscoe New Cut was made in 1820s to permit cargo ships to travel from Lowestoft to Norwich avoiding Great Yarmouth.

57

Reedham Ship Inn. Top about 1870. Bottom about 1890.

Construction of the New Reedham Swing Bridge next to the old single track line. The old line was opened in 1847. The new line was opened in 1904.

View from Reedham looking towards the New Cut, in the centre distance, with the Benns family Raveningham Detached (No 2) Steam Pump on the right of the photograph.

Frozen river at Reedham looking east from the swing bridge in 1954.

Steam boats in the frozen river in the winter of 1928/29 at Reedham with Benns Steam Pump in the background. One boat is 'Gensteam' with a gross tonnage of 31, built in 1924 by Fellows & Co Ltd at Yarmouth for the General Steam Navigation Co of London. In 1931 she became part of the Great Yarmouth Shipping Co. She was often seen towing lighters of coal to Norwich Gasworks.

Today many different types of holiday craft can be seen on the river but catamarans and canoes are rare visitors at Reedham.

Left:
Catamaran 'Mistoffelees' at Reedham 20 March 2009.

Below:
Nicholas Crane in a canoe at Reedham recording a television programme on 23 February 2007.

The river frequently froze in the hard winters of the past. Above: 'Ramble' at Reedham Swing Bridge 28 February 1929, from J. Baker. Below: 'Rose-Julie M' in ice at Reedham in the 1950s. This was one of Metcalf Motor Coasters Ltd vessels. She was built in 1941 and had a gross tonnage of 402. Supplied by Arthur Edwards.

BRICKMAKERS' ARMS

Located on the Reedham Riverside at the foot of School Hill on Mill Road, the Brickmakers' Arms was adjacent to the riverside Maltings and near to the riverside sheds where the bricks were kept awaiting transport by wherry. The brick field where the bricks were made was at the top of Mill Road. The Maddison family were the owners of both the pub and the maltings at one time, and were also at the same time the Reedham brickmakers.

This pub was probably a beerhouse back in the 1700's. It was marked on the 1825 map.

It was for many years a Steward and Patteson house. After closure in 1914 it became a dwelling house.

Date	Licensee / Occupant	Notes/ BRICKMAKER'S ARMS
1836-56	Richard Goffin	Victualler. Brickmakers' Arms. Age 55, Innkeeper & Carpenter in1851.
06.01.1857	Charles Hall	Age 51, Licensed Victualler & Boatwright in 1881.
18.03.1889	Henry Jones	Age 47 in 1891.
13.03.1905	Henry William Clarke	
07.11.1910	Harry Jacob Carter	
06.11.1911	Benjamin Mutten	
14.07.1913	Walter William Pegg	
17.11.1913	Charles Alban Prior	
1914	**Closure**	Licence refused 30 September

LORD NELSON

This is located on Reedham Riverside near the foot of Middle Hill. When it was first built is not certain, but it obviously was given its name in celebration of Admiral Lord Nelson victories at sea sometime in the early 1800's.

A building was shown here on the 1825 Map of the River Yare. The map does not indicate what the building was used for. On the Tithe Map of 1841 the building was numbered as area 428, listed as 'house and yard', and the owner was marked as Mary Ely and the occupier as Edward Goffin. Once again the use that was being made of the premises is not specified, but it was by now certainly a beerhouse.

Date	Licensee / Occupant	Notes/ LORD NELSON
1825	Edward Goffin	Probably the victualler.
1836	William George	Listed as victualler.
1836	Edward Goffin	Listed as 'Beerhouse'. Probably the under-tenant for W. George.
1841-58	Edward Goffin	Innkeeper, age 45in 1841.
1861	James Hall	Age 37, boatwright.
28.09.1891	Mrs Margaret Hall	James Hall's wife
18.10.1892	James Hall	
16.11.1896	Isaac Jones	
13.05.1901	William Cubitt Moore	Age 47, Fish Curer in 1901
30.09.1901	Samuel Halesworth	
17.05.1909	Edward James Harvey	
01.02.1915	Albert Arthur Edward Cox	
07.04.1919	Herbert Edmund Kemp	
16.04.1923	William Weldon James Pit	
22.09.1941	Sidney Mutten	
27.12.1957	James George Findley	
1972	Winifred Joan Findley	Mr Findley died 1972
1985-86	CLOSED	by Norwich Brewery from Dec 85 for 6 months of refurbishment.
1986	William Colthorpe	
1997	Collorick	
2005	Robert Peter Hare	

More boats at Reedham. 'Southern Belle' 9 July 2006. Originally a steamer used as a ferryboat at Plymouth, she was bought by 'Tug' Wilson in 2003 and after renovation used as a pleasure cruiser on the River Yare.

'Hotspur' in the 1950s. This was once one of the Gt. Yarmouth & Gorleston Steamboat Co. Ltd. vessels.

The wherry 'Albion 'at Reedham in 1949 before her sails were tarred. Sonny Horton

Albion was built for the firm of Bungay Maltsters, W.D. and A.E. Walker. She was built as a carvel (flush planked) wherry in oak on oak frames.

Her builder was William Brighton and she was built at his yard on the north bank of Lake Lothing, between Oulton Broad and Lowestoft. Her shed was an old ice house which was demolished after she was launched in October 1898. She cost £455.00 to build. When launched she had a green bottom and a brown oxide top.

Albion's first skipper was Jimmy Lacey, and the mate was his nephew Jack Powley. In 1900 Jack became skipper - an association that would last twenty years.

In January 1929 she sank near Great Yarmouth Bridge, to be raised three days later. In 1931 she lost her mast, and had it replaced with that from Sirius. About this time she was bought by the General Steam Navigation Company, and her name changed to **Plane** and was given George Farrow as master, who kept her trading the Norwich River under sail right up to the war years.

Eventually stripped of all her gear, she became a lighter, and was still doing this work when the Trust found her in 1949.

She sank at Berney Arms on 1st January 1960 and was raised a few days later.

Albion measures 58ft. x 15ft. x 4ft. 6ins. (17.69m x 4.57m x 1.37m), if the rudder is included 65ft. overall. Her registered tonnage is 22.78 and her official number is 148735. The fore and aft rig is carried on an unstayed mast of 42ft. (12.80m), finely counterbalanced at the heel with approximately one ton, allowing for easy lowering of the mast to navigate the numerous Broadland bridges. The mast and counterweight assembly is supported by an enormous tabernacle, braced by tabernacle knees, with the whole supported by the main beam.

'Queen of the Broads' at Reedham. She was 74 ft long with a 13 ft beam, built at Cobholm in 1889 and broken up in 1976.

Mr Rudd at Reedham, skipper of the Queen of the Broads when she made trips along the Yare. Supplied Peter Allard.

Robert Webb on the Reedham Quay. Before WWII he was often seen helping cruisers moor-up. Diane Rushbrook.

Holiday cruisers at Reedham Quay with the Lord Nelson public house on the right.

Inshore minesweeper M2723, HMS Reedham, at Reedham in 1959. She had a length of 107ft. 5 ins, beam of 21ft. 11ins, and a draught of 5ft.

Reedham Quay in 1938 with Sanderson's boatyard on the left. Supplied by Peggy Sawbridge.

Metcalf's 'Daniel M 'in the ice at Reedham in 1954. Supplied by Peter Allard.

More ships in the ice.
'SS Edith' in ice in 1924 near Reedham Swing Bridge. Supplied by Peter Allard.

'Blackheath', the last large sea-going vessels to visit Cantley, returning from the Cantley Sugar factory, laid up at Reedham Quay in the ice in 1997.

REEDHAM BOATBUILDERS.

Lying on the River Yare it is probable that boat building in some form or another has been carried out at Reedham for centuries.

Perhaps the most famous name of the recent past is the **HALL** family of boat-builders. Sometime in the early 1830's a James Hall, who was born about 1787, moved his family from Norwich to Reedham and set up a boat building business here. His sons James and Charles, were both born in Norwich, in 1825 and 1830 respectively, and later they too became boat builders.

The Hall family built many wherries.

Hall's boat-building business come to an end before 1910 and the **REEDHAM DOCK COMPANY** took over the boatyard. This company was also listed in the 1912 and 1916 directories as 'dock owners'. The Reedham Dock Co. Ltd. was started by Mr H. Newhouse and Mr A. H. Newhouse (Newhouse & Co. Ltd.) who were steamship owners and water carriers. Here at Reedham they built a dock 80 ft. by 25 ft. with a concrete bottom and brick sides and which was to provide a site for overhauling, repairing and launching their lighters. The new dock was officially opened on 14th March 1911

CHARLES HENRY HARRIS was listed here in 1925 and 1929 as a boat-builder. Harris built yachts and had a boat hire business at the old Hall's yard.

In 1932 **HERBERT JAMES WALTER SANDERSON** bought the old Hall's boatyard and moved to Reedham from Cambridge.

Rupert 'Tony' Sanderson took over the business from his father. After WWII Tony and his family lived on a converted boat 'Astral' moored alongside the boatyard for many years The Sanderson boat hire and boat repair businesses are now run by **Colin** and **Steve Sanderson**.

Other Reedham boating business during the latter part of the last century were **REEDCRAFT, CORVETTE MARINE** and **PEARSONS.**

REEDHAM FERRY INN TG407015

Standing next to the Reedham Chain Ferry is the Ferry Inn. Buildings have been here since the 1600's and a beerhouse may have been here even back in those early days.

The building is said to have been occupied by the Shepherd family from the early 1700's till about 1773, after when the occupants were the Hoggett family.

Certainly it was a beerhouse when Jeremiah Hoggett was here but after the railway company bought the property in 1844 there is no specific mention in any of the directories from 1845 through to 1869 of this place being an inn, public house or beerhouse. The property was originally part of the manorial lands and belonged to the Lord of the Manor, until it was sold to the railway company in 1844. John Benns became the owner after the railway company and other owners have been the

Reverend T.H. Crossman Day, Mrs G.E. Lockwood, Miss Cooke, the Benns family and the Archer family. The pub was at one time a tied house to Youngs, Crayshaw and Youngs but is now a freehouse.

Date	Occupant	Notes
1807	Mary Hoggett	Occupier renewed lease of Ferry House
1836	Jeremiah Hoggett	Victualler. Ferry.
1841	Jeremiah Hoggett	Innkeeper. Occupier of area 336a: **'Bottle and Glass'**. Owner: J.F. Leathes,
1844		**'Reedham Ferry House'** Property conveyed from Leathes to the 'Yarmouth and Norwich Railway Co. / GER'.
1865	John Benns	Beer Retailer. Location not specified.
1871	John Benns	**Ferry House**. Age 51, Innkeeper.
03.01.1881	George Fowler	**Ferry Inn**. Age 21. Ferryman & Licensed Victualler.
04.07.1884	George Forder	Beer Retailer & Ferryman. **Ferry Inn**, Age 38, ferryman & Licencsd Vict.in 1891. 1895 Advert: 'Boats for Hire & good Fishing in July, August & September'
19.11.1917	Charles Edward Stone	
06.03.1944	Arthur John Benns	
02.01.1950	Norman Archer	
18.12.1972	David Archer	

NORTON BLACK MILL.

This was located on the south side of the River Yare almost opposite 'The Hove' at Reedham, at about TG414014, in the parish of Norton Subcourse, and was marked as **'Black Mill'** on the 1826 map. It was also shown on the 1825 map, the Norton Enclosure map and Faden's Map of 1797. Something is shown here, at area 35, on Norton Subcourse Tithe map of 1841; this is probably the mill but it is not identified. No mill is shown here on the 1880s OS map or on any later maps. This was probably a primitive drainage pump which became redundant by about 1841.

Note: AC Smith suggested there was once another Norton Subcourse mill at about TG408014, which he refers to as 'Reedham Ferry South'. There is, however, no sign of a mill at this location on the old maps.

Reedham Ferry Inn.
Top: showing the ferry in front of the inn and the drainage mill in the distance in about 1904.

Bottom: The inn circa 1950.

COCKATRICE TG405012

This is marked on the 1996 OS map but is no longer a public house.
It is located on the south bank of the river Yare in the parish of NORTON SUBCOURSE at Norton Staithe.

It was not shown on the 1826 Bryant's map, suggesting it may have been built after this date, and was not listed as a public house in the 1836 or 1845 Whites directories. Buildings, however, were shown here on the Tithe map of circa 1841, owned by Rev. Sir Edward Boyer and occupied by Susan Reeve and others.

The name was given as STAITHE HOUSE in 1851 and THE COCKATRICE in 1854. It was marked as the Cockatrice on the c.1886 OS map and all later OS maps.

It was a beerhouse leased to STEWARD & PATTESON and closed in about 1910.

Licensee / Occupier	Comments (**Cockatrice**)	Dates
SUSAN REEVE & Others	Rev. Sir Edward Boyer is owner.	1841
STEPHEN SHEPPARD	age 50 in 1851.	c1850 - 1856
JAMES WIGG	& coal merchant 1861, (coal merchant & farmer 1871)	c1858 - 1871
JAMES SHEPPARD	Staithe Dam, age 51 in 1881, Innkeeper & coal merchant	c1875 - 1888
THOMAS KNIGHTS	& coal merchant	1890 - 1892
HERBERT GEORGE GALER	& coal dealer	1896 - 1908
HERBERT CUSHION	Farmer at Staithe Farm	1912 - 1916
GEORGE CALVER	Motor Haulage Contractor, Staithe Farm	1937

NORTON DRAINAGE MILL

This is located on the south side of the river in Norton Subcourse parish at about TG403011. It is marked on the 1996 OS map. It was marked on the 1886 OS map and all later maps.

It was not shown on the Tithe Map of circa 1841 or the earlier Bryant's map.

It is said to have been built in 1863 according to A.C. Smith. It is a 4 storey tarred redbrick tower mill about 30 feet to the top of the brickwork. The wall thickness at the base is 22 ½ inches. The outside diameter of the tower at ground level is 20 ft 4 inches and at the top is 12 ft 6 ins. A redbrick electric drainage pump, which stands nearby, took over the drainage.

The mill was converted in the 1980s to be used as accommodation. For many years a conical iron roof was in place but in 1997 a new boat-shaped cap was fitted by millwright Richard Seago.

The present owner is Michael Saunders and in recent years the mill has been used as a holiday let.

MTB102

Motor Torpedo Boat 102 was designed by Peter du Cane in 1936 and built in 1938 at Vospers. She took part in the Dunkirk evacuation. After the war she was sold off and converted as a private motor cruiser. She was again sold some years later for conversion to a houseboat.

It was later acquired in 1973 for the Brundall and Blowfield Scouts.

It was refurbished and used in 1976 in the film 'The Eagle has Landed', and also appeared in other films.

Length 68 ft, beam 14'9", draft 3'9" wooden hull with a top speed of about 48 knots.

In 1996 she became the property of the MTB102 Trust. In recent years she was often moored at Corvette Marine, one of the sponsors of the Trust, in Reedham as seen in the photograph taken 9 July 2006.

NORTON STAITH MILL

This was shown with this name on the 1826 Bryant's map at about TG402008 near the junction of Boyce's Dyke with the river Chet. It was marked on the 1825 map as **Norton Common Mill**. It was marked on the Norton Subcourse Tithe map of circa 1841 at area 185 labelled as 'mill', occupied by Richard Nursey and owned by the Drainage Commission. It was also shown on the Noron Enclosure Map as 'Staith Mill'.

This was described by AC Smith in 1989 as ' Derelict tarred redbrick tower Mill reduced to 2 storeys with shallow conical roof and once had a scoopwheel.'

Some marshmen in Norton Subcourse who may have looked after the Norton drainage pumps include:
1881 Census; William Reeve, age 52 on Low Road, James Reeve snr., age 57 and James Reeve jnr., 32 on Nogdam End.
1900 directory: James Reeve, cowkeeper & marshman, and William Reeve Jnr., cowkeeper & marshman.
1922 directory: Robert Edwards and W. Reeve.
1937 directory: Charles Hammond.

Left : Norton Drainage Mill and the modern redbrick electric pump house in May1989. Right Norton Staithe Mill in 1989. From A.C. Smith,.

Reedham Ferry Inn circa 1950.

View from the top of Reedham Ferry Mill showing the Ferry Inn on the right, the Norton drainage mill in the distance and the building that was once the Cockatrice public house in Norton Subcourse.

Reedham Chain Ferry circa 1960. The ferry is pulled by a motor on board the ferry.

Reedham Ferry circa 1910 supplied by Michael Browne. The Ferry public house is shown on the left and the Ferry Mill on the right. The ferry is being hand cranked by the person on the ferry.

Norton Drainage Mill in full working order circa 1930s. Supplied by Sonny Horton.

HARDLEY CROSS

The point at which the River Chet branches off the River Yare is the ancient boundary of jurisdiction between the City of Norwich and the Borough of Great Yarmouth. For hundreds of years the aldermen met here every year in a colourful annual ceremony, known as the 'Hardley Inquest', to declare all the 'abuses and privileges' related to matters of trade on the River Yare. The Hardley Cross was erected here in 1543.

Hardley Cross, where the Chet flows into the Yare, was repaired in 1820, 1884 and in 1899 when the fence was erected around it. The Cross marks the boundary between Great Yarmouth and Norwich where a civil ceremony was held each year.

Hardley Cross at the confluence of the Chet and theYare at about TG400011.
Supplied by Michael Gunton.

GODDARDS'S MILL

This was marked at about TG 400011 on the 1826 Bryant's map on the south of the Yare and to the west of the Chet in Hardley parish.

It was also shown on the 1825 map with the name John Goddard alongside. The land alongside was the property of T. Beachamp Proctor.

It was not shown on Faden's Map of 1797.

On the Hardley Tithe Map, circa 1840, area 127, at this location, was listed as 'Mill Yard' occupied by Mrs Goddard and owned by William Beauchamp Proctor. It is probable that since the mill itself was not mentioned in the Tithe Apportionment that it had already been removed.

It was not shown on subsequent OS map.

ADAMS MILL

Located at about TG396018 on the south of the Yare on Hardley parish and marked on the 1826 Bryant's map.

It was also marked on the 1825 map with the name John Adams alongside. The land here was owned by T Beauchamp Proctor.

The mill was marked on the Hardley Tithe map of 1840 at area 115 and labelled as 'Mill & Yard'. Owned by William Beauchamp Proctor, it was occupied by William Crisp.

No mill was shown on the 1797 map.

It was not shown on later OS map.

LIMPENHOE DRAINAGE MILL (EAST).

TG397019

A drain mill was marked here at this location on the 1797 map. A mill was also marked here on the 1825 map with the name marked alongside, presumably the occupier, James Neave, and the land was owned by John Francis Leathes.

It was not marked, however, on the Bryant's 1826 map!

In NRO/STA731, dated 22 Sept 1842, 'Mill House Farm' was given as 306A 3R 3P and the rent was £305. The owner was John Francis Leathes, the Lord of the Manor of Reedham and the farm occupier was James Neave. On the 1844 Tithe Map area 144 was labelled as 'Mill Yard', owned by Leathes and occupied by James Neave. The mill itself was not listed suggesting it had already become obsolete.

When the Reedham Hall Estate was put up for sale by the executors of John Francis Leathes in August 1848 the 'Old Mill Yard' on plot 282 was part of Lot 6 and occupied by James Neave. (NRO/STA703)

The old drainage mill here must have been made obsolete some time after 1825 and demolished.

A 'draining pump', however, was marked here on the 1880s and 1950 OS maps. This may have been a steam drainage pump erected some time between 1848 and 1880.

It was not shown on 1996 OS map.

LIMPENHOE DRAINAGE MILL (WEST).

TG39460190

This is shown on the 1996 OS map, the 1880s, 1928 and 1950 OS maps and on the Tithe map. On the Tithe map area 140, was called 'Mill & Yard', and area 138, 'Cottage'; both were occupied by William Swash and owned by J. F. Leathes.

The mill was not shown on the earlier 1826 and 1797 maps.

The 4 storey tower is about 35 feet to the curb and had an inside diameter of

16 ft at the base with 22 in thick walls. The tower had three internal floors, the top floor having two windows. It is believed the mill had a boat shaped cap and an 8 bladed fantail without a gallery. The four double shuttered patent sails were probably about 10 ft wide with 9 bays of shutters. The drive was via a 19 ft diameter wooden brake wheel to a 5 ft diameter cast iron wallower set on a wooden upright shaft to a second iron wallower driving a 10 ft diameter cast iron pitwheel with wooden teeth and then to a 19 ft diameter scoopwheel on the same axle.

Limpenhoe Drainage Mill (West) 27 September 1995. Peter Allard Collection.

The drainage mill was built by the millwright William Thorold around 1831. The mill was to be paid for by each person in proportion to the acreage of marsh owned that was to be drained by the mill.
The scoopwheel axle bore the legend *W. ENGLAND 1895.*

From an Agreement for the Drainage of a certain level of Marshes lying in Limpenhoe & Southwood in the County of Norfolk we have the following. (NRO/ MC165/6/1.):
Robert Walpole to pay to John Leathes £25 for 1 acre of marshland, part of areas 138 and 140 on the attached map, to permit the building of a drainage mill and cottage.
'That the specification of William Thorold of the City of Norwich, Engineer hereunto

annexed for the erection of a Drainage Mill & Cottage & for making the Drains & Road & other necessary works to be done for the purpose of the said drainage & his contract to perform the same for the sum of £744 is hereby accepted & agreed to by the said parties & that he shall forthwith commence the said works.'

A person must be appointed by a meeting of the parties to manage the mill and the drains.

'As Witness our hand this 15th day of October 1831. John Frances Leathes. H. N. Burroughes, Jer. Burroughes. Agent for Mrs. C. Burroughes, Wm. Blake, Rt. Gilbert, Fras. Drake. his Benj. X Browning mark Rt. Walpole, by Wm. Foster, his agent. W. H. Maddison, Agent for the execrs. of the Late Revd Jno. Emeris.'

In 1989, Arthur Smith reported that the cap base frame remained on top of the mill and the iron windshaft was still in place but without its canister, however the brake wheel had collapsed. The floor beams and all the other machinery were still in situ. The 10 in square wooden upright shaft was in two sections and had chamfered corners. A 10 ft diameter pit wheel with a 8½ in square iron shaft connected to an outside 19 ft diameter scoop wheel over an outer iron hoop, with many of the wooden paddles still in situ.

Some marshmen at Limpenhoe from the directories include:
1922: Walter Newson at 'The Mill'.
1937: Ernest Charles Mallett.

HARDLEY DYKE
This joins the river at about TG391017.
The present dyke was dug around 1830. The dyke is privately owned and used as moorings for private sailing craft.
An earlier dyke had existed nearby in medieval times.

STAITHE HOUSE
This was Located at TG388011 in HARDLEY at the end of Hardley Dyke.
This was a BEERHOUSE but has long been closed.
It was shown as **THE CHEQUERS** on the 1880s OS map.

Licensee / Occupant	Notes / STAITHE HOUSE	Date
WILLIAM BELWARD	age 67 in 1851	1836 - 1851
SARAH BELWARD		1854 - 1856
JAMES BELWARD	& farmer 10 acres, & maltster age 34 in 1861. (Also listed in 1854 as coal agent at the Staithe.)	1858 - 1877
LYDIA BELWARD		1879
JAMES BARBER	Age 42 in 1881 Licensed Victualler. (& cow keeper & maltster).	1881 - 1892
WILLIAM TAYLOR		1896

HARDLEY DRAINAGE MILL
TG387024

An early windmill was shown on the 1825 map in Hardley parish with the names Timothy Coleman and John Marcon Esq. marked alongside. A windmill was also shown here on the 1826 Bryant's map and labelled as **Hardley Mill**. This mill was located at about TG387022. It was not shown on Faden's map of 1797.
No mill was marked for Hardley on the 1847 map,
No mill was shown on the Hardley Tithe map of 1840. The land where the present mill is located was in 1840 called 'Common Allotment' and was owned by William Beauchamp Proctor and occupied by Samuel Goddard.
The early mill must have become obsolete sometime before 1840.

The 1880s OS map shows **'Hardley Drainage Pump (Wind)'** at about TG387024 located further to the north of the earlier mill.

This later Hardley drainage mill was built as a 4 storey red brick tower, some 43ft to the curb. In 1988 Arthur Smith recorded that the frame remained on top of the tower and the brake wheel was visible but there was no windshaft. The turbine was also still in situ inside the mill.

A stone plaque was set in the wall at second storey level that read *TWBPB 1874*. The initials are those of the one time Lord of the Manor Sir Thomas William Brograve Proctor Beauchamp bart and the date of construction 1874.

The mill was built by Dan England of Ludham. It operated till about 1950 when it was tail-winded and became badly damaged and was then left to fall into ruin. A modern electric pump was built nearby for draining the marshes

A.C. Smith says the date-stone / plaque was removed sometime between 1976 and 1989, but it has since been replaced.

The Mill was leased to Peter Grix in 1985 and restoration was started in about 1991 with the help of volunteers. In recent years it has been fully renovated with millwrights Vincent Pargeter and Richard Seago doing some of the work, and in March 2008 a Visitor Centre was built alongside.

Hardley Drainage Mill in 1989 from A.C. Smith.

Hardley Mill with Cantley Sugar Factory in the background. Top: Postcard view with mill in working order. Bottom: 15 November 2009 after restoration.

86

LANGLEY MILL
TG388025

A modern redbrick electric pump house is located here, only a few yards to the north of the Hardley Mill.

A drainage windmill was marked at about this location on the Langley Tithe map of 1838.

The 1847 map marks this as a '**steam engine**', and a '**draining pump**' was marked on all subsequent OS maps from the 1880s to 1950s at about TG388025 in Langley parish.

On the Langley Tithe Map of 1838 Thomas Burton was listed as the occupier of areas 213, marsh house & yards; 211, mill yard; and 210, mill marsh, and Thomas Beauchamp Proctor was the owner.

The 'pump' on the later maps was immediately to the south of the mill shown on the Tithe map indicating the windmill was replaced by a pump.

The earlier 1826 map indicates that the windmill was perhaps even further north, nearer to ROUND HOUSE, and located at about TG388028 at that time indicating that another previous mill had existed. The mill was also marked on the 1825 map with the name Thomas Burton as occupier and Thomas Beauchamp Proctor as the landowner.

The 1767 map also shows a mill hereabouts again with the landowner William Beauchamp Proctor.

ROUND HOUSE
TG388028

This was shown on Faden's Map of 1797.

It was marked on 1825 map as '**Devils Round House**' with W. Crisp as the occupier.

It was also shown on Bryant's 1826 map as '**Devils House**'.

It was marked on the Tithe Map of 1838.

It was marked on the 1847 map as '**Devils Round House**'.

Marked on 1996 OS map as '**Round House**'.

This is said to have been called Devils House because it is reputed to have fallen down shortly after it was built!

The house was occupied by farmer Robert Burgess in 1937.

CANTLEY East PUMP

A mill was marked here on the 1825 map, but it was not marked on the 1826 Bryant's map! The mill was not marked on the 1837 Cantley Tithe Map. On the tithe map the area where the mill was marked on other maps was at the junction of areas 173, 174, 181 and 182 which were owned by William Alexander Gilbert and occupied by William High. Areas 173 and 174 were listed as 'Mill Marsh' and 'Great Mill marsh'.

A mill was, however, again marked here on the 1847 map. It is probable that the mill on the early maps became obsolete by about 1826 and was rebuilt sometime before 1847.

The draining pump mill was shown on the 1880s OS map and on the 1908 OS map at about TG384034.

The last mill here was still standing, but had no sails in 1901 when the adjacent land was put up for sale.

This mill was a brick tower mill with cloth sails and drove a scoopwheel, and is believed to have been in operation in 1886.

On the OS map circa 1928 the Cantley Sugar Factory was here and the pump was not marked.

CANTLEY BOATHOUSE SITES

In 1901 when the Cantley Grange Estate was put up for sale the stretch of land to the east of the Red House Inn was put up for sale as 'boathouse sites' (NRO/PD291/28).

Initially 35 plots were for sale, 22 of them between the Red House Inn and the east Cantley Pumping Mill, and 13 to the east of the mill. Plots 13 to 16 went to Alexander Pope, plot 7 to Everitt and plots 8 & 9 to Clarkson. Both Everitt and Clarkson were members of the Norfolk and Suffolk Yacht and Sailing Clubs Association which had often had regattas on the river at Cantley. Plots 1, 2 and 6 were also sold. (NRO/PD291/29) The remaining 12 plots between the inn and the pumping mill were again put up for sale at the Royal Hotel, Norwich, by auctioneers George Fitt & Co. Ltd. on 29 June 1901.

Some of these plots became later Woods & Newstead boatyard.

WOODS & NEWSTEAD BOATYARD AT CANTLEY

This was located to the east of Cantley Red House on some of the boathouse sites near to the site of the east Cantley Mill. This was listed in 1908 as Woods & Newstead 'Yacht Builders'. In the 1916 and 1922 directories Ernest Louis Woods and John Walter Newstead were both separately listed as 'yacht builders' at Cantley. There was no boat-builder listed in the 1929 directory.

CANTLEY SUGAR FACTORY

Cantley sugar factory has a special place in the history of this country's sugar industry. Built in 1911/2, it was the first British beet sugar factory.

In the 1916 and 1933 directories it was called 'THE ENGLISH BEET SUGAR

COMPANY LTD.'. The directors included Van Rossum and Dr A Wijnberg.

For many years the beet was delivered here on wherries by river and by rail, but in more recent years the beet and sugar products are transported by road. Until the turn of the last century large coasters delivered fuel to the factory but the last large vessel was in about 2000.

Construction workers at Cantley Sugar Factory. Supplied by Janet Church.

British Sugar pays about 925 growers supplying beet to the factory about £35 million a year. Around £430,000 is paid in business rates.

Cantley factory employs a permanent workforce of about 118 rising to 155 during the processing campaign which lasts, on average, about 155 days. The factory operates 24 hours a day throughout the campaign.

The factory processes in excess of 1.3 million tonnes of beet every year. On average 370 lorry loads are accepted each day. The factory can process up to 10,000 tonnes of beet a day, with an average daily throughput of 9,000 tonnes.

Around 1,200 tonnes of crystal sugar are produced every day. Sugar is stored in six silos, each with a storage capacity of 10,000 tonnes. In addition to the crystal sugar, a further 30,000 tonnes of sugar is produced as a syrup which is further processed throughout the year.

Along with granulated sugar and caster, other speciality sugars are supplied for use as ingredients by the food industry. Granulated sugar is supplied in bulk and in sacks. Caster and the other speciality products are supplied in sacks.

About 80,000 tonnes of sugar beet feed, a high energy animal feed in pellet form, is produced each campaign. This is sold under the Trident Feeds label.

LimeX45 is produced each campaign and sold to farmers to correct acidity, add nutrients, and improve the structure of the soil. Topsoil is also produced for farmers to enrich soil quality on farm and for use in the building industry.

The factory can provide all its own electricity with a generating capacity of 13Mw. Daily fuel requirements during the campaign include 120 tonnes of heavy fuel oil and 150 tonnes of coal.

In 2009 the factory was given permission to expand production for processing imported sugar cane

Cantley Sugar Factory circa 1920. The factory was closed briefly during part of WWI.

REEDCUTTERS. CANTLEY

This was show as **RED HOUSE INN** on the 1880s OS map at about TG382034.
It was an alehouse and had a FULL LICENCE.
It was named as **RED HOUSE HOTEL** in the 1908 directory.
It was renamed in about 2004 as the **REEDCUTTERS**.
It was not marked on the Cantley Tithe Map of 1837, and the area upon which it later was to appear, was then area 185, listed as 'Reed Meadow', without any buildings, owned by William Alexander Gilbert and occupied by John England junior. The Inn must have been built sometime after 1841.

Top; 'Hustler' at Cobholm in January 1975.
Bottom : 'Vagabond' and 'Hustler' at Cantley on 31 December 1974.
Peter Allard Collection.

Some owners from the licence registers include: **WILLIAM ALEXANDER GILBERT** , **E. LACON & CO LTD** from 17.08.1898, **WHITBREAD,** and it later became a **FREEHOUSE.**

Licencee / Occupant:	Notes / Comments	Date
	Pub Not Listed.	1836 & 1837
	Pub Not Listed in census.	1841
JOHN ENGLAND	age 52 in 1851 Publican & waterman: victualler at **Red House** in 1854. (Only a waterman in 1841.)	1851 & 1856
WALTER THOMAS CROWE	& wherry owner	1858 to 1880
ARTHUR JACOB GOLDSPINK	Innkeeper Age 38 in 1881 Alfred listed in 1883!	22.11.1880
JAMES WILSON		19.01.1891
ABRAHAM GEORGE WRIGHT		09.03.1894
WILLIAM PETER JUNIPER		11.03.1895
BENJAMIN AMBROSE COLLINS		18.11.1895
THOMAS WILLIAM PEART	**Red House Hotel** & boatowner in 1908.	01.01.1906
JAMES BANHAM		01.01.1917
THOMAS WILLIAM PEART		19.11.1917
EDWARD HENRY HAMMOND		07.11.1927
JAMES JENNINGS		26.04.1937
BERT NELSON		11.04.1950
FREDERICK WARMAN		20.09.1954
HAROLD MARSHAL LOWE		10.11.1958
EDWIN JAMES CORNELIUS JONES		23.05.1960
EDWIN CHARLES GRAVES		04.06.1962
MARJORIE PHYLLIS GRAVES		14.01.1963

The local Post Office officially opened at the public house on the 3rd April 2000. The latest owners of the pub are Mick Cottrell & Phil Cronin.

Cantley Red House on the left, from a postcard circa 1904. On the far right is Cantley East Drainage Windmill without sails. The Black buildings are Woods and Newstead Boatyards and the white building is on one of the other boathouse sites. Most of this is now the site of the Sugar Factory.

WHITE HOUSE: CANTLEY.

This was shown in CANTLEY on the 1826 Bryant's Map near the river and near the location of the public house now called the RUSHCUTTERS. The exact location, however, is uncertain.

It was also shown earlier as the 'STAITHE HOUSE' at about this location on Faden's 1797 map.

The Norfolk Chronicle of 29th April 1820 carried an advert:-
'Cantley WHITE HOUSE - Situated on river, half way between Norwich and Yarmouth, with the Staithe thereto belonging............ An excellent meadow of 6A 0R 14P with the Common Allotment included............ a most desirable property situated for Brewers, Malsters and the Corn Trade - Apply to Mr Samuel Mitchell, land agent, Norwich'

The Norfolk Chronicle of 22nd July 1820 reported on a theft of coals from the wherry 'Accommodation' moored at the White House at Cantley on 10th May 1820. The coals were put into a bin owned by **Edward Layton**, proprietor of the White House.

The 1837 Cantley Tithe map shows at area 225 'Cottage & Garden' owned and occupied by John England senior. This was at about the location of the White House, but it was not named or listed in the Apportionment as a public house.

(No other property was shown near this location as a public house on the tithe map, suggesting there was not a public house near the river at that time.)

This area is now the location of the local sewage works.

The 1847 map also shows 'Cantley White House, Stables & Garden', near the river, with owner William Alexander Gilbert and the occupier as John England junior. This may be the Red House Inn and not the original White House, but it was John England senior who was the publican at the Red House!

THE YARE — CANTLEY.

A postcard view of the river circa 1911 showing Cantley Red House on the right.

MARSH FARM Cantley.

This is located at about TG379035 .

On the 1837 Tithe Map this was marked at area 192 as 'Cottage and Garden' occupied by Charles Layton and John King and the owners were the Trustees of Charles Layton.

The occupant here in 1854 was listed as Samuel Curtis, in 1881 the occupier was Samuel W. Curtis, a marshfarmer of 100 acres, age 31, and in 1908 was Richard Lambert Curtis, brother of Samuel W Curtis.

The Curtis family were responsible for the drainage of the marsh land and probably operated the Cantley West Drainage Pump. NRO/MC513/103, dated 1854, gives the cost of 8 years drainage of the marshland by, or for, Richard Curtis as £12.

CANTLEY (WEST) MILL

A MILL was marked at about TG376030 on Bryant's map of 1826. It was also shown on the 1825 map with the name William Henry Gilbert alongside as the landowner.

The 1837 Tithe map does not show a mill here, but area 197 adjacent to the mill site was given as 'Mill Marsh' owned by William Alexander Gilbert and occupied by William High. It is possible that the windmill had become redundant before the Tithe map was drawn up.

The document NRO/Spe549.316x4, dated 3 September 1846, mentions the sale of Cantley Mills:

The highest bidder to be the buyer. Two bidders make an auction. Any dispute over the Mill to be put up again.

A deposit of 25% to be placed at the fall of the hammer. The residue of the purchase money to be paid previously to the delivery of the materials.

The mill to be taken down at the purchasers expense and removed on or before the expiration of 2 months from this date if required by the Commissioners.

Should the mill not be removed by that date, to be resold and the deficiency if any in such second sale to be made good by the defaulter at the present sale.

Purchase Price £70

Deposit £17-10s

Residue of £52-10s to be paid on 2 November.

Signatures

W.A. Gilbert.

John Green.

John Denny Gilbert.

It is probable that this document refers to the removal of the this old drainage mill, ready for the steam pump which was built near here and was shown on the 1847 map as a 'Steam Engine'.

NRO/MC513 mentions the 'Cantley Engine', presumably located here, and indicates that it was capable of 16 horsepower and estimated that it required about 147 tons of coal for working for 153 days at 10 hours per day, over the period from March 1856 to 1857.

The 1880s OS map shows a Drainage Pump at about this location. The pump is also marked on the circa 1908, 1928 and 1950 OS maps.

The Reedcutters at Cantley in 2009, formerly the Red House.

Cantley Sugar Factory in 2009.

LANGLEY DYKE.
This runs from about TG369029 in a south westerly direction from the right bank of the river.

Also sometimes referred to as the Holy dyke, Langley dyke was cut in medieval times to allow stone to be brought from the River Yare to build a Benedictine abbey, the remains of which can be seen in among the private farm buildings near the end of the dyke. In later centuries the narrow, shallow waterway continued to be used by wherries to bring in essential supplies, and take out goods for trade.

WHERRY INN
This is located in the parish of LANGLEY at about TG365026, near the end of Langley Dike.

This was not marked on the 1826 Bryant's map, suggesting it was built after that date.

It had a FULL LICENCE.

It was supplied by **STEWARD & PATTESON** during the year November 1837 - 1838. Copyhold was owned by **FINCH & STEWARD** from 1837 - 1851. Later owners were **WATNEY MANN** and it was later a **FREEHOUSE.**
It closed in 2003, and was offered for sale as `The former Wherry Public House '.
It remains closed to this day.

Licensee / Occupant	Comments/ Notes	Dates
JOHN HALL	age 56 in 1851.	1836 - 1856
MOORE CUMBY	Publican & marsh drainage engine driver & blacksmith Age 68 in 1881.	1858 - 1888
GEORGE POTTER		1891 - 1900
SAMUEL FRARY		1908 - 1912
ARCHIBALD LAMBERT CURTIS		1916
GEORGE LEVI OWEN		1922
JOHN PREECE		1925
EMANUEL THORPE		1929 - 1937

LANGLEY DRAINING PUMP (WEST).

A draining pump is marked on the 1996 OS map at about TG363037 on the right bank (sw side) of the river in Langley parish.

This was marked as a 'steam engine' pump on the 1847 map, and it was marked on the 1880s map as a 'draining pump'. The landlord of the Wherry Inn, Moore Cumby, operated the pump at one time.

Nothing was shown at this location on the 1838 Tithe map, the 1826, 1825, and 1797 maps, suggesting a steam pump was sited here sometime between 1838 and 1847. The latest pump here is electric.

FLEET DIKE
This joins the river at TG361045 and runs in a northerly direction.

The Wherry Inn at Langley.

Construction of the War Memorial near the Wherry Inn. Supplied by Michael Gunton.

BUCKENHAM FERRY DRAINAGE MILL TG353045

A windmill was marked on the 1767 map near this location and the landowner was William Beauchamp Proctor.

A drainage windmill was also marked on the 1826 map near this location. A mill was also shown on the 1825 map with the name Benjamin Waters and the landowner as Thomas Beauchamp Proctor.

The tithe map, however, indicates that the drainage windmill was located at a different position at about TG355045, some distance to the east of the position of the current mill. This was on area 101 labelled as 'Mill & Yard' occupied by Benjamin Waters and owned by William Beauchamp Proctor. A 'cottage & garden' on area 102 was where Benjamin Waters lived.

The 1880s OS map shows **two** draining pumps at TG353045, one marked as 'wind', so the other was probably a steam pump. These two pumps were positioned immediately adjacent to where the cottage occupied by Benjamin Waters stood.

The current Buckenham Ferry drainage mill standing next to the River Yare, was built as a 4 storey red brick tower and had windows on the 1st, 2nd and 3rd floors. By 1989, A.C. Smith reported that, the mill was roofless and had a definite lean. A brick shed had been built against the mill and a modern pump stood

alongside it.

The last man to work the mill was a Mr Ward.

The Army Air Corps lifted a temporary roof onto Buckenham Ferry mill in October of 1993. This was done free as a lifting project for the AAC.

This temporary cap of corrugated iron sheet was destroyed by gales in early 2007.

Buckenham Ferry Drainage Mill in 1989. A. C. Smith.

Buckenham Ferry Drainage Mill 25 August 1938. Peter Allard Collection.

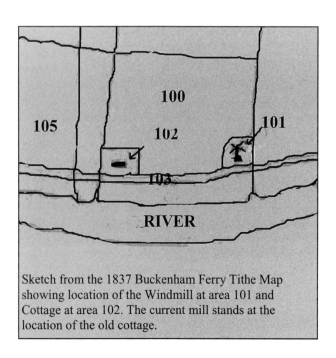

Sketch from the 1837 Buckenham Ferry Tithe Map showing location of the Windmill at area 101 and Cottage at area 102. The current mill stands at the location of the old cottage.

Buckenham Ferry Mill on 12 December 1994. Supplied by Peter Allard.

The BUCKENHAM HORSE SHOES

This was Located in the BUCKENHAM FERRY district at about TG349050.

A building was shown at about this location on the 1767 map.

It was shown on the 1825 map as **BUCKENHAM HORSE SHOES** with occupier John Jay. '**THE HORSE SHOES**' was marked at area 129 on the 1837 Tithe map shown as 'Public House and Staithe' occupied by John Jay. It was then owned by William Beauchamp Proctor. It was also marked on the 1847 map as **HORSE SHOE** Public House with John Jay as the occupier

On the 1864 map of the Langley Estate it was called '**THE HORSE SHOES INN**' and occupied by Charles Layton.

It was an alehouse and had a FULL LICENCE.

It was closed by 1872 and had become a private house according to the licence register.

It was a **FREEHOUSE** supplied by Steward & Patteson.

Licensees:	notes	date
JOHN JAY	& carpenter	1825 - 1847
CHARLES LAYTON		1851 - 1869
JOHN GARRETT		1871

BEAUCHAMP ARMS (BUCKENHAM FERRY HOUSE)

This is located in the parish of CARLETON ST PETER on the right bank of the river.

BUCKENHAM FERRY HOUSE is recorded as being mortgaged by Thomas Berney to Thomas Palgrave in 1704.

The 1767 map marks a building here, and the landowner was shown as John Berney.

It was shown on the 1797 map as the **FERRY HOUSE**.

It was leased in 1806 by Thomas Trench Berney to Thomas Orchard, and Conveyed by Thomas Trench Berney to Sir Thomas Beauchamp Proctor in 1815,

It was granted from Thomas Beauchamp Proctor to William Beauchamp Proctor in 1819.

'**THE FERRY**' is marked on the 1825 map with JEREMIAH FISH.

On the Tithe Map of 1839 '**BUCKENHAM FERRY HOUSE**' is shown on area 1 occupied by Sarah Fish and owned by William Beauchamp Proctor.

The 1847 map shows **FERRY PUBLIC HOUSE** with the owner as William Beauchamp Proctor and the occupier as Sarah Fish.

On the 1864 map it was called Buckenham Ferry House and occupied by John Fish.

In 1881 census it was referred to as **FERRY HOUSE**.

It was called the **BEAUCHAMP ARMS** in 1883 and 1890 and again after 1982. It was named after the Proctor Beauchamp family who once owned land on both sides of the river, in the area where the ferry operated.

It was put up for sale on 16th July 1938 with Ireland auctioneers at the Royal Hotel in Norwich:-

'The fully licensed Riverside Hotel known as Buckenham Ferry 'The Beauchamp Arms'. A recently built Brick and Tiled House with large Club Room, 2 Public Bars, Bar Parlour, ample living accommodation. The extensive premises include Stabling, Cow Houses, Barn etc. Also the Prescriptive Ferry together with the Chain Ferry Boat with Landing Quays the whole extending to 7a 3r 21p, Garden, Pasture Land etc. The well built Brick &Tiled Fully Licenced Hotel .... With a frontage of approximately 450 feet with Quay Heading.
The house contains Ground Floor Front Entrance Hall 2 Public Bars, Coffee Room, large Club Room 35' x 18', Private Sitting Room or Bar Parlour, Kichen, Larder. First Floor 4 Bedrooms, Dressing Room, Bathroom and WC. Second Floor 5 bedrooms and 2 cupboards. Good Cellar.........Good Well of Water...........For the past 40 years has been leased to Messrs Bullard & Sons whose lease expires at Michaelmas.'

It had a FULL LICENCE and was leased by Bullard & Sons for many years. It is now a FREEHOUSE.

The Ferry House at Buckenham Ferry from an old postcard. Supplied by Michael Gunton.

Licensees :	Notes	Date
Mr LLOYD		from 1785
Mrs HUMPHRIES		undated
THOMAS ORCHARD		from 1806
JEREMIAH FISH		1825
JOHN FISH		1836
SARAH FISH		1839 1851
JOHN FISH	age 44 in 1861 & farmer of 45 acres	1854 - 1865
JOHN GARRETT	age 37 in 1881 & farmer 27 acres	1869 - 1896
JAMES GEORGE GIBBS		1900
WILLIAM THOMAS ROYAL		1904 - 1908
WILLIAM HUBBARD		1912
ALFRED CHARLES STEWARD		1916 - 1922
HERBERT GEORGE SANDWELL		1925
HERBERT ROBERT CORNISH		1929
ARTHUR MALLETT		1933 - 1937
Mr ROBERTS		undated
Mr HOLLAND		undated
Mr CHATER		by 1956
PERCY NICHOLS		late 1950's ?
FRANCES NICHOLS		to 1998
RAY HOLLOCKS	(Tapestry Taverns)	1998 -

Buckenham Ferry

The horse ferry across the river ran from the Ferry Public House (Beauchamp Arms) across the river to Buckenham Ferry Parish. It was marked on the 1797 map and all subsequent maps. It was last used just after WWII.

In 1938 when the pub and ferry were put up for auction the ferry boat was described as a chain ferry boat 31 ft by 16 ½ ft. The ferry boat charges were at that time:

Passengers	1 ½ d
Cycles	3 d.
Motor Cycles	6d.
Horse & Cart	6 d.
Motor Car	1s 0d
Wagon & Horses	1s 0d.

During the WWII years a floating pontoon bridge was placed here by the army.

THE YARE — BUCKENHAM FERRY.

A post card view of the Ferry at Buckenham. Supplied by Michael Gunton.

There was a sailing club near Beauchamp Arms.

CLAXTON DRAINAGE MILL

A mill was located at about TG346052 according to Rex Wailes. This he said had a scoopwheel and the sails were by England.
No mill was marked here in 1826.
The 1880s OS map shows a 'draining pump' at about this location.
Billy Mason maintained the drainage pump in the 1920 and 1940s when it was a Ruston oil engine.
No mill is shown on the 1996 map, but another mill called 'Claxton Drainage Mill' is marked at TG330040 near the end of Claxton Fleet on the 1996 OS map.

CLAXTON NARROW GUAGE RAILWAY

From about 1926 to 1936 a narrow gauge track was laid from Claxton Manor Farm to the river bank a short distance to the west of Claxton drainage pump. The engine was a converted old 1914 Model T Ford which pulled trucks loaded with sugar beet.

ROCKLAND BROAD

On the right bank of the river at TG340052 is '**Short Dike**', and at TG340058 is '**The Fleet**' which both run in a west-south-west direction into Rockland Broad.

Rockland Broad is the graveyard for several old wherries: Star of Hope, Gleaner, Unexpected, Diligent, Chieftain, Providence, Cambra, Madge, Tiger, Empress, Leverett and Myth, all sunk here during WWII.

In 1908 a Mr Botterell proposed a ship canal between Gt. Yarmouth and Norwich and suggested that Rockland Broad should be expanded to 400 acres and become a naval base.

ROCKLAND LONG'S CORNER DRAINAGE MILL

This was located near Rockland Broad and Short Dike at about TG335050 in Rockland St Mary. It was shown on the 1880s OS maps as 'draining pump'. It was not shown on the 1839 Tithe Map.

Rockland Long's Corner drainage mill is believed to have been a skeleton mill.

OLD SCIENTIFIC

A colourful local character who made his living on Rockland Broad was Jimmy Fuller - alias 'Old Scientific'.

For much of his life Old Scientific lived aboard a houseboat on Rockland Broad. He was famed locally for his wildfowling skills.

When the author T.H. Emerson met him during an adventure in the Broads he had just shot two ospreys, one with a three-pound pike still in its talons.

NEW INN

Located in the parish of ROCKLAND St. MARY at TG328046

On the Tithe Map of 1839 the 'New Inn Public House' is listed at area 68 adjacent to the brick ground kilns on area 67. It was owner by Robert Gilbert Snr. and occupied by Michael Reeder at that time.

This was a **FREEHOUSE** supplied by Steward & Patteson during the year 1837/38 and again in 1845/46. It was later a **YOUNGS, CRAWSHAY & YOUNGS** house (Leasehold by 1897) then **BULLARDS, WATNEY MANN, BRENT WALKER** and then **PUNCH TAVERNS** in 2004.

Licensees	Comments/Notes	Dates
MICHAEL REEDER		1839 - 1850
WILLIAM WATSON	Age 36 in 1851 & coal merchant	1851 - 1875
HENRY SAYER	Age 62 in 1881 & coal dealer.	1877 - 1896
S. SAYER		1897
JOHN MAYES		1900 - 1908
JAMES GEORGE GIBBS		1912 - 1916
E. H. HAMMOND		1922 - 1925
WILLIAM FISK		1929
FREDERICK WILLIAM FISK		1933
HENRY STEPHEN BREACH		1937
WYNN & ERNIE CURSON		1975

BRICKWORKS
There were brickworks at Berney Arms, Reedham and both Surlingham and Rockland St. Mary.

Rockland St Mary
The Rockland St Mary Tithe Map of circa1839 indicates several places in the parish associated with brick making:

Area on Tithe Map	Landowner	Occupier	Description
10	Robert Gilbert jnr.	James Browne	Brick Ground
169	Robert Gilbert jnr.	Robert Gilbert & James Browne	Brick Ground Sheds
139	Rev. Robert Long	John Diggins	Clay Brick
156	Robert Blake (Later Robert Horace Chandler (1842))	Robert Blake (Later William Page)	House Kilns & Sheds, (later House & Old Kilns)
111	John Colman	John Colman & John Youngs	House Brick Kilns
67	Robert Gilbert Snr.	Robert Gilbert Snr.	Brick Ground Kiln

In 1836 Robert Gilbert, Robert Blake and J. Crowe were listed as brickmakers.

In 1845 Robert Gilbert and Robert Blake were listed as brickmakers.

In the 1854 directory the Rockland Brickyard was listed as belonging to Robert Gilbert Jnr of Ashby Hall and John Rudd was the brickmaker.

In 1866, 68 & 69 John Rudd is again listed as Brick and Tile manufacturer and as a coal merchant.

The 1883 & 1908 directories list William Wade Stanley at Rockland as 'brick and tile maker'.

Eventually Lacey & Lincoln Ltd took over the Rockland brickworks and were listed in 1916

Surlingham

There were two separate brickworks in Surlingham in the mid 1800s, one operated by Gibbs Murrell of Lessingham House and the other by Samuel Barnes.

The Gibbs Murrell brickground was sold in March 1861.

The 1847 Navigation map shows 'Rockland Brick Kilns' by the river at about TG303066 in Surlingham parish. This is where Barnes brickfield was located close to the church. The staithe here was often referred to as 'Surlingham Brickyard Staithe'.

The 1866 and 69 directories list Barnes as a Brick Merchant.

The 1881 census returns for Surlingham list Samuel Barnes at Manor House as a 'farmer and a Brick Manufacturer' employing 25 people at the brickworks. He is again listed in 1900 as a Brick & Tile Maker. Barnes brickfield closed in about 1907, and no brick maker was listed in 1908.

Barnes owned two wherries 'Herald' and 'Meteor'.

DISUSED STUMPSHAW DRAINAGE PUMP.

A 'disused pump' was marked at TG331066 on the 1880s OS map on the left bank of the river in **Strumpshaw**. It was not marked on the c.1908 OS map or later maps
It was not marked on the 1797 Faden's map.
It was not shown on the Tithe Map of 1846. The land here in 1846 was owned by Richard Henry Vade Walpole and Reginald Henry Neville and occupied by Thomas William Gilbert.
This was probably a stream drainage pump erected sometime after 1846.and derelict before 1880!

COLDHAM HALL

This is located on the right bank at TG324072 in SURLINGHAM parish.
This is believed to have been built originally in the 18th century as a shooting lodge.
Legend has it that the name was given to it after Queen Anne on a trip down the river stopped here briefly and requested food, and was given a meal of cold ham.
It was shown on the 1767 map with this name and marked with the land owned by Thomas Beevor. It was also marked on the Faden's 1797 map as Coldham Hall.
It was shown on the 1825 map with Tompson as the owner. On the Tithe Map of 1843 the building was marked on area 338 and labelled as 'House & Yards', the owner on the Tithe Apportionment was listed as Charles Tompson Esq. and the occupier as Richard Gostling.
It was marked on 1847 map with owner John Brandram Morgan and occupier Robert Gostling.
It had a full licence.

Some owners from the licence registers were: **CHARLES KETT TOMPSON & HENRY KETT TOMPSON, MORGANS, BULLARDS, and WATNEY MANN.** The present owners are CRITERION ASSET MANAGEMENT.
It was conveyed from the Tompsons to John Brandram Morgan & Walter Morgan 25th March 1845 along with 3a 22p. Tompsons, however, reserved the right to use the boathouse.
The schedule stamped 10 March 1845 says the tenant was Richard Gostling and the property was late in the possession or occupation of JOHN HOWSHAM. (ref . NRO/BR160/6)
On 2nd May1911 (ref NRO/MC14/402) 'All the Furniture & Effects, Stock-in –Trade, Outdoor Effects, Garden Requisites, Marquee, Yacht, Pleasure Wherry & Fittings, Sailing and Fishing Boats' of Coldham Hall Hotel were put up for sale by auctioneer Hanbury Williams.
The pleasure wherry was the '**The Leisure Hour'**. This wherry had been owned by George Grimsell and had previously been named 'Bessie'.
Some modernisation was carried out in 1974.

Licensee	Notes	Date
CHARLES LAYTON		1820
JOHN HOWSHAM		Unknown
RICHARD GOSLING	age 63 in 1851	1836 - 1851
CHRISTMAS FRANCIS	victualler	1854 - 1856
ROBERT FRANCIS	& Ferry	1858 - 1871
EDWARD BROWN	Age 32 in 1881. & corn merchant & fishing boat & ferry proprietor	1875 - 1890
GEORGE FISHER		1891 - 1896
CHARLES TOWSER		1900
GEORGE GRIMSELL	Age 54 in 1901 living in Reedham.	1904
EMMELINE GRIMSELL	Widow of George Grimsell.	1908
ALBERT CHARLES GODWIN		1912
SAMUEL CHARLES GIBBS	& boatbuilder. (also listed as boatbuilder in 1908)	1916 & 1922
WILLIAM JAMES BREACH	Proprietor & Yacht Builder & designer; engine repairs & overhauls, motor cruisers & yachts for hire.	1922 & 1937
HARRY LAST	Note he founded the Coldham Hall Sailing Club in 1951.	1938 - 1973
DAVID & BETTY PUGH		1975
	Closed in early 2009	
DAVID & DEBBIE LINDER		2009-10

Strumpshaw Pump 20 September 2009 from Peter Allard.

View by Coldham Hall in 1947 from Peggy Sawbridge.

GOLDEN GALLEON (ML162)
Photographed near Coldham Hall on 16 July 1997 by Peter Allard.

She was a Fairmile 'B' motor launch, ML162, built by A.M. Dickie & Sons of Bangor in about 1942. After service in WWII with the Royal Navy she was transferred to the Royal Netherlands Navy and continued in service for two more years.

She was sold and converted into a passenger boat around 1950. Based at Great Yarmouth she made pleasure trips along the Yare, usually only as far as Reedham.

She had a wooden hull. Length 107.4ft Breadth 18.6 ft Draught 4.6ft.
Tony Martin was the owner at one time, and the last owners was Tapestry Traditional Taverns who acquired the vessel in 2000 but failed to keep her running and she was left rotting at Reedham at the entrance of the New Cut till she was eventually striped of superstructure and the hull towed to St Olaves for disposal in 2006.

FOOT FERRY at Coldham Hall.

A ferry operated between Colham Hall and Brundall and was marked here on the circa 1880 OS map. Until about1955 a rowing boat foot ferry ran here. A bell was located on the Brundall side of the river to alert the ferry operator that there was a customer waiting to come across the river.

YARE NAVIGATION RACE

This race is run in September of each year.
It starts at Coldham Hall and the competitors go downriver to Breydon Water and back.

YARE HOTEL

Located at about TG328079 on the left bank of the river in Brundall, close to the Brundall railway station is the Yare Hotel.
This was not a public house in the 1881 census when it was called 'Bleak House'.
It became a public house around 1883.

Some owners have included:

H FLOWERS & Co. of Brundall when it was an Off Licence.
STEWARD & PATTESON then took the Lease and a full licence was granted on 29th August 1892.
STEWARD & PATTESON purchased the property in 1931, and they were later taken over by **WATNEY MANN**. on 21 February 1967. It was closed by Watney Mann (East Anglia) Ltd on 29.09.1970.
After closure it was soon re-opened as a freehouse and **G. D. FISHER** became owner on 1 March 1972 according to licence register.
It was briefly renamed '**QUEEN ELIZABETH**', and it was again renamed the **YARE** in about 1978.

Licencee / Occupier	Notes	Date
H Flowers & Co. (Owners)	The Yare Yachting, Boating and Angling Station	1888
JAMES HENRY FAWCETT	Yachts, boats and pleasure wherries for hire	29.08.1892
GEORGE SMITH		03.05.1897
ALBERT WILLIAM LINFORD		01.05.1899
JAMES HASTINGS		13.05.1901
ARTHUR JAMES NEWSON	Yachts & rowing boats for hire	13.01.1908
ELLEN OCTAVIA NEWSOON	Fine £1 plus 4/- costs or 14 days detention for being open during prohibited hours 28.09.1914. Fine £5 plus 24/- costs or 28 days detention for permitting drunkenness 14.12.1914	08.09.1913
EDWARD HENRY REEVE		12.04.1915
HILDA ADA REEVE		20.11.1916
EDWARD HENRY REEVE		07.04.1919
HILDA ADA REEVE		08.01.1923
CHARLES LOUIS DAVIS		04.01.1926
WILLIAM JOHN KNAPP		01.01.1951
ARTHUR CHARLES MORE		22.12.1958
DONALD LESLIE MANN		02.11.1964
GEOFFREY DODDING		12.10.1970
GEOFFREY DAVID FISHER		17.01.1972

BRUNDALL BROAD.

This was a private broad located at about TG319082.
In 1925 and 1926 it was put up for auction (NRO/BR241/4/686 & MC14/261,389x1). It included two boathouses between the river and the broad, a luncheon hut, bathing hut, ornamental grounds, orchard and Osier beds and a total of 11 acres.

BRUNDALL GARDENS

This was created by Dr Beverley who bought the land here to the west of Brundall Broad in 1881.
Mr Frederick Holmes Cooper bought the gardens in 1919.
In 1933 it was bought by the Stringer family, and in 1968 by Michael Aspin

THE RIVERSIDE HOTEL

Riverside Hotel at Brundall Gardens. Supplied by John Baker

This was built in 1923 by Mr Holmes-Cooper on the river's edge and on the Brundall Gardens.
On 28 August 1945 **Riverside House Hotel** Brundall (NRO/BR241/4/1431)

116

was put up for sale by auction at the Royal Hotel in Norwich. It was described as follows:

Ground Floor: Entrance Lounge, Smoke Room, Sun Parlour, Lounge 18ft by 12 ft, Dining Room 25ft 9in by 18ft, Ladies and Gents cloakrooms, Servery, Larder, Storeroom, Scullery, Store Cupboard, Tradesman's Entrance, Managers Room, Office and Luggage Entrance.

First Floor: 12 bedrooms and 2 bathrooms.

Second Foor: 4 bedrooms.

Includes a Garage 41ft x 26 ft., at the rear is a Yard, Workshop, Wash-house and Store Shed. Also includes a Yacht Basin and meadowland.

In August 1993 it was struck by lightning and destroyed by fire.

As the holiday trade faltered the hotel fell into disuse.

It was renovated in the 1970s by Colin Chapman and used as offices.

BRUNDALL GARDENS STEAMSHIP COMPANY.

This was operated between the two war years and they owned the S.S. VICTORIOUS. This ran holiday makers to and from the Brundall Gardens from Great Yarmouth.

BRUNDALL BOAT YARDS

Brundall is today a busy boating centre. Many boating businesses began here in the late nineteenth and early twentieth centuries as holidaying on the rivers and Norfolk Broads began to become popular.

Some boating businesses include:

Brooms boats: John Charles Broom listed in 1908 as Boatbuilder. This had previously been the Norfolk Broads Yachting Co boatyard and prior to that George Mollett had a boatyard here.

The Cole family started a boating business here in 1953 called 'TIDECRAFT CRUISERS'. The Cole family businesses expanded to include boat building and hiring, riverside stores and chandlery.

Bell Boats began about 1950 and a marina was made in the late 1950s. The company built boats and operated a hire fleet. They also ran a pleasure launch called 'Brundall Belle' for a short time.

Several boating businesses are located along the Brundall Bay Marina and Hobro's Dyke. These include Eastwood Marina, Yareside Marina, VIP Harvey Eastwwod, Willow Cruisers, Freshwater Cruisers, Fen Craft, Alpha Craft, Bees Boats, Bucaneer Boats, Harbour Cruisers, Silverline Marine, Classic Marine, Alexander Cruisers.

Tom Allard in 1956. Tom Allard had a tea stall at Bell Boats, Brundall. Supplied by Peter Allard.

HOBRO'S DYKE

This is named after J.S. Hobrough who bought the land here in the 1920s and cut the dyke and developed the site for mooring plots.

BRUNDALL BAY MARINA.

This was made in 1990 by the Funnell Group.

RIVERSIDE RESTAURANT

This was opened by Ken Taylor in about 1951 on the site of the owners Bell Boats Ltd. at Brundall.

Norman Chalk had the restaurant licence from 26 July 1965, and then on 8 November 1971 Michael Vernon Gosling took over the licence.

In the mid 1980s it was used as the clubhouse for the Brundall Motor Yacht Club.

FERRY HOUSE
TG308076 SURLINGHAM

Marked on the 1767 map was the **FERRY** and the landowner was Sir Randal Ward. It was shown on the 1797 map as **SURLINGHAM FERRY**.

In 1808 a settlement of estates by Neil Earl of Roseberry and Archibald John for the Inn called Surlingham Ferry with the Ferry (NRO/MC410/1,745x4).

It was marked on the 1825 and 1847 maps as **Surlingham Ferry** and as being occupied by Samuel Parker and owned by Lord Roseberry.

On the Tithe Map of 1843 it was marked on area 230 as '**Ferry House**', owned by Lord Roseberry and occupied by S. Parker.

It has a full licence and some later owners include **YOUNGS, CRAWSHAY & YOUNGS; STEWARD & PATTESON** on leasehold; **BULLARDS** by 1960; **WATNEY MANN and ADMIRAL INNS**

It is believed to date from before 1725, and is said to have ice storage facilities in the 1700s. Two dates appear on the building: 1725 and 1876 indicating it was modified and added to.

The horse ferry here was marked on the 1767 map and operated until WWII. The last ferry was built by Breach at the boatyard at Coldham Hall.

Surlingham Ferry circa 1880. Christopher Davies.

Licencee	Comments	Date
SAMUEL PARKER	victualler, age 78 in 1851 & farmer	1825 - 1869
Mrs MARY OXLEY & SAMUEL PARKER	Ferry House	1836 &1845
JAMES CHAPMAN	tax collector, coal merchant & victualler	1875 - 1877
HENRY FREDERICK CHAPMAN	Age 27 in 1881& farmer of 50 acres	1879 - 1890
GEORGE TIBBENHAM		1891
JOHN PLANE		1892 - 1896
HENRY RAWSTONE		1900 & 1908
ALBERT EDWARD TEMPLE		c1912 - c1918
JOHN S. HOWARD		1922
WILLAM POWLEY		1937
HERBERT WHITMORE		1953 to 1976
SUE & DEREK SLATFORD		2005-2006
SONIA COX		

POSTWICK DRAINAGE PUMPS.

Two drainage pumps were marked on the marshes in Postwick on the 1880s O.S. map at about TG303074 and TG 303070. These were not shown on earlier maps and were probably steam pumps.

SURLINGHAM PUMP.

A drainage pump was marked on the 1880s O.S. map at about TG304071. No pump or mill was shown on the earlier Tithe Map. This was probably a steam pump.

WOODS END INN

This is located in the parish of BRAMERTON at about TG290062.
It has a FULL LICENCE and is now a FREEHOUSE.
Part of the frontage dates from 1885, other parts are older.
It is believed to have been built before 1700.

It was supplied by STEWARD & PATTESON from 1837 to 1842 and it was later taken over by **MORGANS,** then **BULLARDS** circa1961, and **WATNEY MANN** in about 1963.

On the 1767 map **WOODS END HOUSE** is shown with the name of Mrs Perry alongside.

It was marked as **WOODSEND** on the 1797 map.

On the 1825 map it was again marked as **WOODS END** but with the occupier as Mathew Purland and the proprietor as John Cullins.

It was listed as **WOODS INN** in 1836, and put as **WOOD'S END FERRY** in 1845, and on the 1847 map it was marked as **WOODS END,** and it was given as **WOOD'S END FERRY** tea gardens & pleasure grounds in 1854, suggesting there was a ferry crossing here at that time.

It is marked on the 1996 OS map as **WOODS END TAVERN.**

This was a regular stopping place for pleasure boats coming from Norwich in the early twentieth century and Billy Bluelight used to race the boats back to Norwich.

Water skiing is often seen on the wide stretch of river near this public house in the summer months.

An old view of Woods End Inn supplied by Michael Gunton.

Woods End Inn in 2009.

Licensees / Occupier	Notes / Comments	Date
Mrs PERRY	Possible owner.	1767
MATHEW PURLAND	occupier	1825
THOMAS BALDWIN	victualler WOOD'S INN,FERRY	1836
SAMUEL TURNER	victualler & plumber& painter glazier: age 36 in 1851: ferry 1858.	1845
JOHN FRENCH		1864 - 1877
EDWARD YOUNGS	Age 43 in 1881 & ferry owner	1879 - 1883
HENRY WILLIAM FLAXMAN		1888 - 1892
HENRY CARVER		1900 - 1904
FRANK SCARLE BINGHAM		1908
HENRY KNIGHT		1912
WILLIAM BLANCH		1916 - 1922
ALBERT BLANCH		1925
GEORGE H TAYLOR		1929
RUSSELL EDMUND DIGBY	run by Mrs Ivy Digby during WWII	1933 - 1957
CHANCE		c1957
ERNIE & WYNN CURSON		1968 - 1973
PETER TALLOWIN		1973
Martin		2007– present

Billy Bluelight

In the 1920s / 30s Billy Bluelight used to challenge boat trippers to races along the river bank between Norwich and Bramerton. He was famed for his claim "My name is Billy Bluelight, my age is 45, I hope to get to Carrow Bridge before the boat arrive"

Dressed in cricket cap and running gear, this small, wiry man would challenge vessels to a race. His real name was William Cullum and he made a living selling flowers and cough sweets in Norwich's Gentleman's Walk. A supporter of the Temperance Movement, Billy stayed '45' for many years: living until his nineties.

Postcard of Whitlingham Reach from Peter Allard Collection.

Jarrold series postcard 7670 with pleasure steamer 'WaterFly' near the White House, just visible between the trees, at Whitlingham, from Peter Allard collection.

Top: Everard's 'Signality' and 'Scarcity' at Whitlingham Reach in March 1956.
Bottom: Everard's 'Spirality'. Peter Allard Collection.

DRAINING PUMP KIRBY MARSH

A **Windmill** is shown on the 1825 map near the boundary between Whitlingham and Kirby Bedon at the end of the dyke at about TG 283072. The names on the 1825 map are Edward Lombe and Robert Corby. It was also shown on the Tithe Map.

WHITLINGHAM MARL PITS

The 'marl pits' were shown on the 1843 Whitlingham Tithe Map as area 5 owned by Edward Lombe Esq. and occupied by Robert Corby. The 1847 map again shows Edward Lombe as the owner and John Wortley as the occupant.
Chalk from the workings was taken down river to cement works at Berney Arms and Burgh Castle.

In the late 1800s and early 1900s pleasure boat trips often took day-trippers to Whitlingham so they could explore the chalk tunnels and the lime kilns.

WHITLINGHAM SEWAGE FARM

Following an act of Parliament in 1867 for improving 'the severing of Norwich' a small sewage farm was located at Whittingham and has been considerably extended and modified over the years.

POSWICK VIADUCT

This was constructed in about 1990 as part of the A47 trunk road which crosses the river at about TG282082.

WHITE HOUSE TG 267078

This is located in TROWSE NEWTON at the boundary with Whitlingham parish.
It was also known as the **WHITLINGHAM WHITE HOUSE.** The '**White House**'
was marked on the 1797 Faden's map. It was also shown on the 1825 map as
'Whitlingham White House'. It was marked on the 1880s and 1996 OS maps as
'White House'.

The Trowse Newton Tithe Map, of circa 1840, shows at area 63 '**Public House & Garden**' with the occupier as Archibald Money.

The 1854 entry for Whitlingham Parish says that the house is actually in Trowse Parish and includes a ferry connection across the river Yare.

The entry in the directory of 1864 states that the house 'has recently been pulled down and its site attached to the mansion at Crown Point.'

The 1868 directory states that Robert John Harvey Harvey was having a splendid mansion erected near the site of the demolished White House Tavern. This new building was also named the White House but was not a public house. R J H Harvey was the Lord of the Manor of Whitlingham for some time and owned all of the Whitlingham parish lands

The Public House was supplied by Stewards during the years 1844 to 1845 and from 1847 to 1848.

Some occupants include:

Licensee / Occupant	Comments	Date
JAMES KING	White House Ferry	1836
ARCHIBALD MONEY		c.1840
ANN KING	Whilingham White House Ferry	1845
JOHN WORTLEY	Whitlingham White House Tavern age 45 in 1851. (Note he was also the occupier of Whitlingham Chalk Pits on the 1847 map.)	1850 & 1854
R DIGBY		1858
MARY ANN DIGBY	& farmer	1861
Benjamin Parsons	agricultural labourer. White House	1871

Thorpe Gardens Inn circa 1880 by Christopher Davis. Now the Rushcutters.

RUSHCUTTERS

Located by the river in Thorpe St Andrews at 46 Yarmouth Road this pub was formerly known as the **HINSBYS GARDENS** and then the **THREE TUNS,** then **CATTERMOLES GARDENS** and became **THORPE GARDENS INN** on 01.09.1879.

It was damaged by enemy action 09.05.1942 and again 20.09.1944.

It became the **BOAT & BOTTLE** between 1968 to 1985 and then the **RUSHCUTTERS** on 16.09.1985.

This was according to the licence registers an alehouse, and some owners were YOUNGS & Co, then STEWARD, FINCH & PATTESON, then STEWARD & PATTESON and later a WATNEY MANN house from 21 February 1967 and then Schooner Inns Ltd. on 14 April 1969.

Licensee / Occupant	Notes (RUSHCUTTERS)	Dates
JOHN BORE		1783
WILLIAM LAKE HINSBY	Three Tuns in 1836	1836
JOHN WARD		1839
THOMAS JOSEPH CATTERMOLE		1850
ROBERT CATTERMOLE		1851
MARY CATTERMOLE		1854
JOHN HART	Age 52 in 1881 Convicted in 1885 of keeping open during prohibited hours.	circa 1869
BARNABAS BUCK		05.10.1885
HENRY GUITON CHASTON		11.11.1889
WILLIAM GEORGE WARD		15.01.1912
KATHLEEN WARD		13.01.1913
EDWARD CHARLES GRAY		25.11.1935
HAYDEN HEPWORTH		15.08.1938
EDITH ETHEL HEPWORTH		09.02.1942
PHILIP ANTHONY LOWELL		08.09.1952
RICHARD WILFRED BROOKE		11.11.1957
PATRICIA J. HULL		25.03.1968
FREDERICK R. BRAMPTON & DAVID T. MORGAN		14.04.1969
FREDERICK R. BRAMPTON & PETER ANDRE GNAEGI		24.11.1969
TURNELL	Protection Order	29.09.1971
FREDERICK R. BRAMPTON & NICOLA CARLO MAZZARELLO		08.11.1971
RICHARD GAVIN MACLELLAN & KEITH PARSISSON		19.06.1972
THOMAS DEREK SHIMMELL & KEITH PARSISSON		17.12.1973

Thorpe Gardens in about 1907. Supplied by John Baker.

HART ISLAND

Hearts Cruisers are located here. The Island is named after John Hart the one time landlord of the Thorpe Gardens Inn.
In 1908 J Hart & son was listed as 'boat and yacht owners'.

NEW CUT TG264083 to TG 254082

This was cut to allow shipping to continue up river to Norwich in about 1844 when the Norwich to Great Yarmouth Railway line was constructed with low bridges over the river.

WHITLINGHAM BROAD

A recent broad created from the Gravel Pits which were here. The gravel extracted here around 1989 was used in the construction of the new A47 road bridges nearby. Three new Broads were the result and these are used for recreational activities.

Trading wherries and boatbuilding on the Yare by Michael Sparkes.

Trading wherries plying the River Yare brought prosperity to the city of Norwich sailing up to the Second World War. Boatbuilding was another industry found on the river. Mike Sparkes Archivist for the Norfolk Wherry Trust also one of the volunteer skippers of the trusts trading wherry "Albion" explains his family ties with both industries.

Mike Sparkes sailing 'Albion' built in 1898.

Since the mid 1980s I have been researching wherries and my family's connection with these vessels. At that time I was lucky to glean information from my grandmother Lily Carr born in 1892, her late husband Stephen worked on the Norwich River with his father, also a wherryman, who skippered the wherries 'Go Forward', 'Caroline', 'Ramona' and 'John Henry' for the Hobrough River Contractors based at Thorpe.

Lily's Husband Stephen   Stephen's Father

Lily also said Stephen's Grandfather and Great Grandfather were boat builders near Norwich, after some research I found Stephen Field's boatbuilding yard was at Thorpe on the Whitlingham side of the rail-bridge close to the Rush Cutters Public House. The yards slipway can still be seen there today. Stephen Field built 2, 5 and 6 ton Broads Yachts around 1860s/70s first in Norwich then later in the 1880s/90s at his Thorpe yard where he also built the steam wherry 'Empress'.

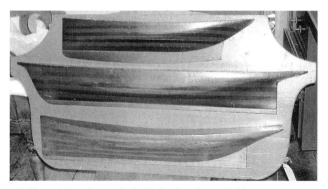

Half models of vessels built by Stephen Field.

During my research in the 1980s I contacted my uncle Stephen as I knew he had been a waterman like his father also working at the Hobrough Yard at Thorpe St Andrew. Later in 1987 Stephen joined the Norfolk Wherry Trust to again acquaint his self with his past and again sail on a trading wherry. At that time I asked Stephen to write down his memories of life on the river.

'A Few Memories of the Broads Wherries. 1921 – 1934'.

Having recently become a member of the 'Wherry Trust' reaching the age of 73, retired, I have been able to spend a week or two each year on Cruising on the Broads; unfortunately Arthritis prevents sailing.

Seeing the 'Albion' swanning around, brought back memories of my childhood on the Broads with my grandfather, Stephen Field, or 'Sling' as he was known among the wherrymen.

My earliest memories are of my mother nursing my brother George, I would be about five years of age and my brother around three months, mother would be sitting on the Dead Hatch by the Tabernacle, as we sailed past the Stracey Arms Pub.

Memories are fading a bit now, but I remember such people as Tyrell, Cates, Billy Tooley, Royal, Bunn, Gedge, Rump, Bircham and Crow, also wherries 'Emily', 'Ella', 'Maude', 'Rambler', 'Lady Violet', 'Widgeon', 'Bramble' and the 'John Henry'; my Grandfather was skipper of this wherry.

I particularly remember Billy Tooley as a rather rotund and jolly man. Other memories are of wherries passing with the shout of 'There you go then' and any information that might be of use to them on their journeys passed on. Also seeing the Coaster 'Alacrity' making for Thorpe Power Station, and of stopping overnight at Coldham Hall, having a bottle of Ginger Beer and an Arrowroot biscuit in the bar whilst my Grandfather had his pint. Playing on the swing and catching minnows from the pub ferryboat, with Billy Breach's daughter who was a couple of years younger that me. I was about eight years old. Leaving Coldham Hall just before dawn for Yarmouth Coal Yard.

I also remember being awakened by the sound of my Grandmother (who always accompanied my Grandfather) getting the ashes and cinders from the fire grate to put on the Plankway so that Grandfather did not slip when using the quant, and the Tap, Tap, Tap of his feet and the swish of the Quant as he walked forward for another Set. Looking out of the Cabin Light seeing the frost on the river banks and trees, all the sounds were very crisp and clear.

Stopping at Buckenham Ferry for a while, and raiding the Plum Trees in the pub garden, whilst Grandfather had his pint of beer.

Passing the chainferry at Reedham. The iron motor wherry 'Petty' was passing making for Norwich with 'High Pockets' and his son on board.

As we approached Breydon Water my Grandfather always insisted that I was up and dressed, for negotiating round to the Bure, making for Potter Heigham where I received many a tanner from old Herbert Woods, whilst tied up at the bridge waiting for the tide to drop.

Once my Grandfather missed the posts at the Coal Yard at Yarmouth where he wanted to wait for the tide to change, to go up to Breydon. The wherry, I think it was the 'John Henry', took the Ebb tide on the low and away we went down the harbour towards Southtown Bridge. My Grandmother was at the tiller, my Grandfather was waiting to get a line to somewhere. He managed to get the line to a moored drifter but the line was cut by the 'Yarmouth Bell', a pleasure steamer coming up the harbour. We drifted under the bridge and managed to tie up to an Estonian Schooner a few hundred yards from the harbours mouth.

We left on the flood tide next morning. We heard later that a Seaman on the schooner had murdered another seaman during the night that we were tied to them.

There are many more memories but now most have gone. One that came to mind, when at the age of fourteen, whilst working on Hobrough's dredger at Ludham Hall in 1930. The skipper sent me across the river to fetch some beer from the Ludham Dog pub. On returning to the row boat there it was gone! Apparently a motor cruiser had gone past, so I got on my bike (which was kept at the farm while we were working) and went to Horning Ferry. The village constable was there, I told him that the cruiser being the only boat passing the dredger probably pinched the row boat. So we waited until it appeared, and sure enough it was towing the row boat. The constable and myself got into a dingy and went to the middle of the river and stopped it. The crew admitted taking the row boat, because their dingy had been sunk. The constable made them tow me, my bike and the row boat back to the dredger.

The last memory was working for Hobrough pile driving at the Steam Navigation Wharf at Norwich aged eighteen. I fell in the drink for the first time on the rivers. This was my last connection with the rivers until after my retirement in 1981.

'Boy Sling'

Wherry skipper Stephen Field " Sling " sitting centre with his wife Jane standing with young Stephen sitting between, their wherry being loaded with sugar beet at Surlingham around 1920s note the broken gaff.

BUCK

This public house is located at 55 YARMOUTH ROAD Thorpe St Andrews and overlooks both the main road and the river..
Some parts of the building are believed to date back to the 17th century.

This is believed to have been the **WHITE LION** till about 1775.

This was an alehouse according to the licence registers and some owners include: St Georges Brewery, Youngs & Co. from about 1864, Youngs, Crawshay & Youngs, then Bullards. Watney Mann from 4 April 1967, and then the Norwich Brewery. Some occupants include the following:

Licensee / Occupant	Notes	Dates
JAMES SMITH		1830
JOSEPH SMITH	& coal dealer age 53 in 1851 & gardener	1836 - 1861
Mrs M. A. SMITH		1865 - 1869
PHILIP FROST	& brickmaker.	by 1871
FREDERICK TIBBS WILLIAM HARPER	Licence transferred from heirs of late P. Frost	10.07.1876
WILLIAM JAMES HARPER	Age 35 in 1881 & coal merchant	by 1877
CATHERINE HARPER		15.08.1898
WALTER ALFRED MOORE		22.11.1915
WALTER PERCY MOORE		26.11.1934
EDWIN GEORGE ROTTER		10.04.1961
RICHARD THOMAS EDWIN MORGAN		19.11.1962
JACK RICHARD QUINNEY		03.02.1969
PATSY DASHWOOD		1982
VANESSA MARTIN & PETER SCOTT		From June 2005

RIVERGARDEN

Located at 36 YARMOUTH ROAD in THORPE St. ANDREW this public house is said to date from around 1650. It once included a bowling green. It was until recently known as the **KINGS HEAD**. It suffered some damage by enemy action on 29th September 1944.
It was renamed the **RIVERGARDEN** 20th April 2000.

Licensee	Notes	Date
JOHN BUNTING		Circa 1700
ROBERT FRANCIS		1830 - 1845
WILLIAM PROVART	age 50 in 1851	1850 - 1854
GEORGE BAILEY		1856
JOHN DOWLAND		1858 - 1861
Mrs C. DOWLAND		1865
JAMES OUTLAW		1869
WILLIAM PARKINS		1871
WILLIAM PONDER		by 1872
GEORGE BUTCHER		12.07.1875
JAMES PIPE CHANDLER		08.01.1877
GEORGE PYLE		09.07.1877
THOMAS EDWARD WATSON	Age 41 in 1881	06.01.1879
HARRIETT WATSON		27.08.1894
ARTHUR FREDERICK WATSON		01.07.1907
JOHN THOMAS MARTIN		04.11.1907
JOHN HENRY BETTS		08.02.1909
FRANK EDWIN SIMPSON		01.12.1930
ERNEST JOHN NEALE		21.08.1933
EDWARD JAMES CARTER		21.11.1938
VIOLET CARTER		08.07.1957
IVAN CLIFFORD WELCH		02.02.1959
THOMAS FRED TAYLOR		04.11.1963
PETER SYDNEY GOOCH		23.09.1968
JOHN BINGHAM		2008

The BLOFIELD & WALSHAM LICENCE REGISTERS list some owners as **STEWARD & PATTESON,** (Freehold owned by Steward, Patteson & Steward as recorded c1845.) **WATNEY MANN** from 21 Feb 1967, and **WHITBREAD** before 1996.

An extension for a restaurant was built in 1996.

Valentine Series Postcard circa 1908 of Thorpe Reach. Supplied by John Baker.

TOWN HOUSE HOTEL

This is located at 18-22 Yarmouth Road in Thorpe St Andrews adjacent to the river .

Some of these buildings are believed to date back to 1700 or perhaps earlier. One of the buildings located here is said to have once been called the 'Town House', hence the name of the hotel.

This is a 'BEEFEATER RESTAURANT'.

ALAN PEEK obtained a 'residential and restaurant' licence for the premises on 04.11.1963.

At one time in the early twentieth century George Jenner had a boating business here.

The Buck at Thorpe St Andrews circa 2000.

NORWICH POWER STATION

This coal fired power station was located in Thorpe near the confluence of the Wensum and the Yare and was opened in 1926. This was the destination for many of the large seagoing ships carrying coal as fuel for the power station. The coal fired power station has long been gone and was replaced by a gas fired power station, and much of the land here is now available for redevelopment. Large vessels carrying coal stopped coming up river to the power station in the 1960s.

TROWSE EYE

This is the name given to the point at which the river Wensum and the river Yare converge. It is also sometimes referred to Trowse Hythe.

The Yare continues around the southern outskirts of Norwich through Lakenheath, Keswick, Cringleford, Bawburgh, Marlingford, Brandon Parva etc. meandering its way towards its source near Shipdham.

As large boats do not proceed up the remainder of the Yare but instead follow the Wensum into Norwich this is a good place to conclude our journey.

WHERRYMEN.

In the nineteenth century there would have been hundreds of wherries and wherrymen and watermen living by the river and many living on board the vessels.

In the 1881 census returns the following people are only a few of those to be found onboard wherries on census day/night:

At **Surlingham**:

Name	Vessel
Samuel Himes(?), age 71(?) from Upton	Poverdence
George Hurrell, age 22 from Rockland St Mary	Lousia
Aurher H Baldry, age 16 from Gt Yarmouth	Red Rover
Charles Hurrell, age 58 from Berghapton	Express
Horace Hurrell, age 31 from Rockland St Mary	Emma Lucy
And James Hurrell, age 18 " "	"
Henry Jordan, age 28 from Surlingham	Herald

Norton Subcourse:
Benjamin Bessay, age 46 from Gt. Yarmouth	Volunteer

Trowse:
William Breeze, age 34	Shannon
Thomas William Breeze, age 14	"

Reedham:
Joseph Shepherd	Faith
William Shepherd	"
Alfred Powley	Fawn
Charles Beales	Experiment
George Crowe	"
William Howes	Elephant
John Stanlow	"

Bramerton
Joseph Rowlands, 24, from Norwich	Allen
Thomas Wright, 47, from Horning	Marhela
Henry royal, 59, from Norwich	Clipper
Samuel Legister, 52, from Norwich	"
Thomas Chipperfield, 30, from Reedham	Dalia
Charles Beckett, 44, from Norwich	Jane
William King, 24, from Norwich	"

FERRIES

Between Great Yarmouth and Norwich there were no bridges crossing the river, but several ferries were shown on the old maps.
These include:

Seven-Mile House Ferry, Reedham which was marked on Bryant's Map as a foot ferry. This was probably only a row boat and used by the marshman's family to cross the river to the Haddiscoe Island.

Raveningham Ferry near Benn's Steam Pump was marked on Bryant's map as a foot ferry. This was also only a row boat used by the occupants to cross the river to Reedham.

Reedham Ferry was marked on Faden's map and has probably been a crossing point for centuries.

Devil's Round House Ferry was marked on Bryant's Map as a foot ferry.

Buckenham Ferry was shown on Faden's map.

Coldham Hall Ferry shown on the 1880s OS maps.

Surlingham Ferry was shown on Faden's map.

Bramerton Woods End Ferry was shown on the 1880s OS maps.

Whitlingham Ferry was shown on Faden's map .near the White House.

COASTERS

Some of the regular sea-going vessels which travelled the river were large, up to about 500tons. In the 1930s and 50s Everard's '**ity**', and Metcalf's '**M**' boats were frequent visitors. Metcalf's '**M**' boats of 1954 are listed here.

Negotiating the river was not an easy task and accidents were common. Ships often hit the river banks as they negotiated the river bends and smaller craft were frequently hit.

One example in the Evening News of 24th July 1979 was a report of a coaster 'A King I' colliding with two pleasure craft and the Reedham Ferry causing serious damage to all three.

Name	Built	Gross Tonnage	Cargo Type
Anthony M	1944	465	Tanker
Caroline M	1935	1598	Tanker
Eileen M	1938	323	Tanker
Ellen M	1936	534	Dry
Jim M	1944	410	Dry
Lisbeth M	1953	939	Dry
Monica M	1936	354	Dry
Paul M	1938	478	Dry
Peter M	1937	972	Dry
Polly M	1937	360	Dry
Rose-Julie M	1941	402	Dry
Thomas M	1938	507	Dry

MAPS

Some of the maps referred to in the text include:

The 1767 map (ref NRO/Case 16e/108) was prepared by Joseph Rumball jnr. and shows the stretch of river from Langley to Bramerton.

Faden's map of Norfolk published in 1797.

The 1825 map (ref NRO/MC103/47) was produced to illustrate the buildings, with their owners and occupiers, along the river between Norwich and Great Yarmouth, probably as information to back the building of the New Cut between Reedham and St Olaves/ Haddiscoe.

Bryant's map of Norfolk published in 1826.

Tithe Maps, and Apportionments, for the parishes listed land owners and occupiers across the individual parishes. Most maps were first produced around 1840.

The 1847 Norwich Yarmouth Navigation Map (ref NRO/C/Scf1/454) was presented to the House of Lords with a proposal to alter the width and course of the river in numerous locations to improve the navigation for shipping from Gt. Yarmouth to Norwich. Had the proposal come into affect the public houses at Berney Arms, Coldham Hall and Surlingham Ferry could all have been lost.

The 1864 Map of the Langley Estate (NRO/205/2) shows the extent of the estate of the Beauchamp Proctor family and covers land in several parishes beyond Langley.

Ordnance Survey Maps.

YARMOUTH & GORLESTON STEAMBOAT CO. LTD

This company ran the Ferry between Gorleston and Great Yarmouth but many of their vessels also made trips along the River Yare.

The Yarmouth and Gorleston Steam Boat Co. Ltd. was listed in the 1896 directory and subsequent directories. The Secretary was listed in the 1896 and 1900 directories as Frederick Wright. Thomas Bradley was listed as Managing Director in the 1908 and 1922 directories. Leonard Platford was the Company manager in the 1920's

The directories from 1911 to 1937 say:

'……..run a frequent service of steamers between Yarmouth and Gorleston during June, July, August and September: also daily (Sundays excepted) River Trips to the Norfolk Broads.'

Some of their vessels are given here.

Vessel	Number	Tonnage	Built	Hull
Cobholm 20hp screw steamer	YH11 111057	46,21	Fellows Yarmouth 1900	steel 72'4",16'0",7'6"
Gorleston 14hp screw steamer	YH7 104075	56,25	Yarmouth 1895	steel 73'0",16'2",7'9"
Pride of the Yare 14hp screw steamer	YH94 92971	46,21	Cobholm Island 1889	steel 75'7",12'5",4'1"
Queen of the Broads 14hp screw steamer	YH93 92972	42,19	Cobholm Island 1889	steel 69'7",12'1",4'2"
Resolute 17hp screw steamer	YH24 117539	71,32	Millwall 1903	steel 73'0",17'3",8'4"
Yarmouth 14hp screw steamer	YH6 104074	56,25	Yarmouth 1895	steel 74'0",16'2",7'9"
Yarmouth Belle 24hp screw steamer	YH20 92988	48,21	Southtown Suffolk 1892	steel 82'0",15'2",6'1"

YARE AND WAVENEY LIGHTER CO. LTD.

This was formed in 1903 and was managed by Henry Newhouse.
Some of the vessels which would have regularly been seen on the Yare include the following, most of which were registered at Great Yarmouth:

Vessel Name	Number	Built	Tonnage Goss,Nett	Hull: L,B,D
Active 20hp screw steamer	YH1 117553	Kirkintilloch 1903	38, nil	Steel 59' 4", 14' 0", 6' 1"
Alpha 11hp screw steamer	YH23 111067		39, 26	Wood 66' 6", 16' 9", 7' 7"
Bell				
Busy 20hp screw steamer	YH6 104100	Beckingham 1894	42, 15	Steel 73' 0", 16' 7" 5' 2"
Commerce steamer	YH29 117543	Gainsborough 1903	55, 55	
Despatch steamer		Gainsborough 1903	55, 55	
Expedition steamer	YH30 117545	Gainsborough 1903	57, 57	
Forward steamer	YH31 117546	Gainsborough 1903	57,57	
Good Hope steamer	YH35 117549	Gainsborough 1903	60,60	
Handy steamer	YH34 117550	Gainsborough 1903	60,60	
Hannah wherry	YH24 111068		15,15	
Hope wherry	YH8 104109	Ludham 1863	17,17	
Industry steamer	YH32 117547	Gainsborough 1903		
Jack of All Trades steamer	YH33 117548	Gainsborough 1903	60,60	
Keystone Keel/ motor tug	YH21 117570	Gainsborough 1904		
Leader ketch/ motor tug	YH22 120331	Gainsborough 1904	61,58	
Midget motor tug				
Nimble 5hp screw steamer	YH14 120344		3,1	Wood 26' 5", 7' 1" 2' 7"
Onward motor tug	YH13 120343	1905	29,28	
Primrose Motor tug				
Swallow wherry	YH7 104108	Norwich 1860	16,16	
Swift wherry	YH28 92976	Beccles 1865	19,19	
Tiger wherry	YH25 111069		25,25	
William wherry	YH26 111070		25,25	

JAMES HOBROUGH & SONS.

The company carried out works along the river during the early part of the twentieth century and owned several vessels. They had yards at Bishop Bridge, Norwich, and at Thorpe St Andrews, off Griffen Lane and close to the position of the new Postwick Viaduct. Some of their vessels registered at Gt. Yarmouth in 1920 include:

Name	Number	Tonnage	Built	Hull: L,B,D
Bell 10hp screw motor	YH4 125535	21,14	Reedham 1895	wood 57'4",15'6",3'6"
Dora wherry	YH6 125537	25,22	Reedham 1897	
Eight	YH24 120353	33,33		
Five	YH21 120350	29,29		
Four	YH20 120349	25,25		
Hope wherry	YH8 104109	17,17	Ludham 1863	
Maud wherry	YH7 125538	24,20	Reedham 1899	
Shamrock wherry	YH8 125536	27,23	Reedham 1901	
Swift wherry	YH28 92976	19,19	Beccles 1865	
Terrible 8hp screw steamer	YH1 128542	13,3	LimeHouse 1872	wood 40'5",9'2",5'3"
Three	YH19 120348	33,33		
Tiger wherry	YH25 111069	25,25		
Two	YH18 120347	29,29		
William wherry	YH26 111070	25,25		

OTHER VESSELS REGISTERED AT GREAT YARMOUTH

Some other vessels registered at Great Yarmouth in the early twentieth century that would have frequently been seen on Breydon Water and the River Yare include:

vessel	number	tonnage	built	hull	owners
Brit sloop	YH2 137589	4,4	Norwich 1908		Baron Dammers, Brit Hs., Reedham
Gertrude wherry	YH44 125532	29,25	Reedham 1885		Newhouse Ltd. Norwich. Manager: Archie H. Newhouse.
Jenny Lind 20hp screw steamer	YH14 84587	73, 49	Reedham 1883	Wood 81' 1", 17' 7" 4' 8"	Jenny Lind Steam boat Co.Ltd, Norwich.
Hathor Wherry	YH25 125518	23,23	Reedham 1905		Miss Ethel M. Colman, Carrow House.
Kestral 15hp screw steamer	YH12 108398	66, 39	Southampton 1898	Steel 85' 0", 16' 1" 5' 3"	J & J Colman Ltd, Carrow Works, Norwich. Manager: John C Wright, Southtown.
Orion wherry	YH102 104090	20, 20	Coltishall 1894		Arthur Chas Sadd, Loddon.
Sirius wherry	YH92 104082	29, 29	Southtown 1896		Woods, Sadd, Moore & Co.Ltd, Loddon.
Triton wherry	YH5 115544	13, 13	Yarmouth		Aubrey A Blake, The Chantry, Norwich.
Uranus wherry	YH14 104078	27, 27	Yarmouth 1895		Woods, Sadd, Moore & Co.Ltd, Loddon.
Vega wherry	YH13 104077	28, 28	Southtown 1895		Henry Edwin Sadd, Loddon.
Water Fly 25hp screw steamer	YH7 104064	49, 23	Yarmouth 1894	Steel 72' 5", 14' 6" 6' 3"	John F. Long, Cobholm.
Waveney wherry	YH24 92984	31,31	Southtown 1891		Mrs Beatrix M. Simmonds, Woodbury, Farley Hill, Berks.
Widgeon fore & aft rig	YH30 128536	18,15	Wroxham 1898		James G. Gibbs, Rockland St.Mary.

Queen of the Broads. Supplied by Ivan Mace.

Jenny Lind. Peter Allard Collection.

Photographs from Bridget Jex, circa 1952, taken near Reedham Swing Bridge.

BIBLIOGRAPHY & REFERENCES:

Brundall Local History Group, The Book of Brundall & Braydeston, ISBN9781841146300.
K. S. Garrett, Everard of Greenhithe, 1991, ISBN0905617584.
Jack Points, Surlingham: A South Rivers Village, 1990.
Jamie Campbell, The Royal Norfolk & Suffolk Yacht Club, 2009, ISBN 9780903094108.
Jamie Campbell, Hamilton's Navigations, 2001, ISBN0903094088.
Sheila Hutchinson, Berney Arms: Past & Present, 2000.
Sheila Hutchinson, The Halvergate Fleet: Past & Present, 2001, ISBN0954168305.
Sheila Hutchinson, The Island (The Haddiscoe Island): Past & Present, 2002, ISBN 0954168313.
Sheila Hutchinson, Berney Arms Remembered, 2003, ISBN0954168321.
Sheila Hutchinson, Reedham Remembered, 2006, ISBN0954168348.
Sheila Hutchinson, Reedham Memories, 2007, ISBN9780954168353.
Arthur C. Smith, Drainage Windmills of the Norfolk Marshes, 1990, ISBN 0951576607.
Robert Malster, Wherries and Waterways, 1986.
Robert Malster, The Broads, 1993. ISBN 0850338603.
Roy Clark, Black Sailed Traders, 1961, ISBN 0715354434.
A.H. Patterson, Wildlife on a Norfolk Estuary, 1907.
Robert Simper, Norfolk Rivers and Harbours, 1996, ISBN0951992759.
Peter Allard, Maritime Great Yarmouth, 1995, ISBN 1 857700821

Various Documents held at the Norfolk Records Office. (NRO)
Tithe Maps and Apportionments on microfilm at NRO.
Census Records held at Norwich Library.
Kelly's Directories for Norfolk.
White's Directories of Norfolk.
Harrod's Norfolk Directories.

Other books by Sheila Hutchinson:

  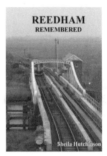

Berney Arms: Past & Present, 2000. (Out of Print)
The Halvergate Fleet: Past & Present, 2001, ISBN0954168305. (Out of Print)
The Island (The Haddiscoe Island): Past & Present, 2002, ISBN 0954168313.(Out of Print)
Berney Arms Remembered, 2003, ISBN0954168321. (Out of Print)
Burgh Castle Remembered, 2005, ISBN095416833X. (Out of Print)
Reedham Remembered, 2006, ISBN0954168348.
Reedham Memories, 2007, ISBN9780954168353. (Out of Print)
The Lower Bure from Great Yarmouth to Upton. 2008, ISBN9780954168360.